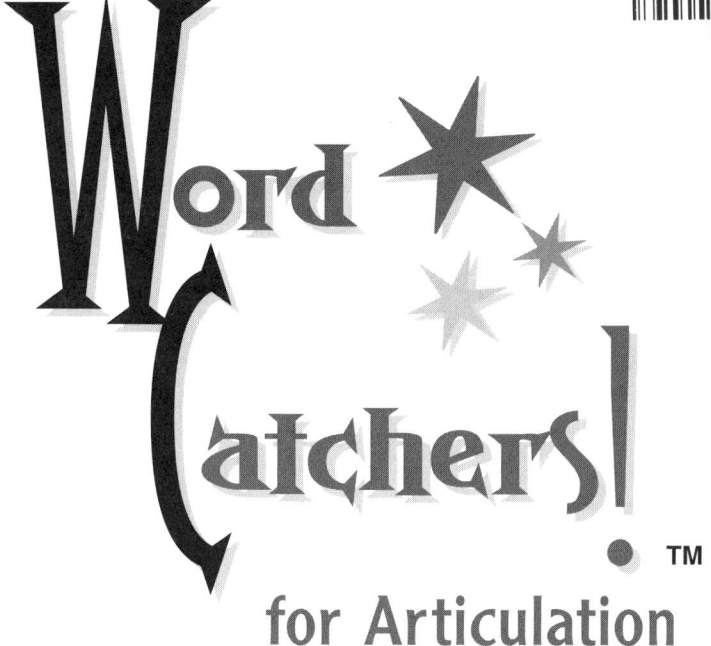

for Articulation

Peg Hutson-Nechkash

Skill Area: Articulation
Ages: 5 through 9
Grades: K through 4

LinguiSystems, Inc.
3100 4th Avenue
East Moline, IL 61244-9700

800-776-4332

FAX: 800-577-4555
E-mail: service@linguisystems.com
Web: linguisystems.com

Copyright © 2004 LinguiSystems, Inc.

All of our products are copyrighted to protect the fine work of our authors. You may only copy the word catchers and forms as needed for your own use with students. Any other reproduction or distribution of the pages in this book is prohibited, including copying the entire book to use as another primary source or "master" copy.

Printed in the U.S.A.

ISBN 0-7606-0538-6

About the Author

Peg Hutson-Nechkash, M.S., CCC-SLP, is a speech-language pathologist for the school district in Barneveld, Wisconsin. She received her Bachelor's degree in Communicative Disorders from the University of Wisconsin–Madison and a Master of Science degree from the University of Wisconsin–Eau Claire. Peg is the author of numerous books and a game.

Word Catchers for Articulation is Peg's first publication with LinguiSystems.

Dedication

To Sam and Tim

Illustrations

Original illustrations by Margaret Warner
Some images © 2004 www.clipart.com
Cover design by Chris Claus

Table of Contents

Introduction 5
Making Word Catchers 7
Blank Word Catcher 8
Homework Helper Letter 9
Progress Log 10

Initial S 11
Medial S 21
Final S 30
S Blends 40

Initial L 50
Medial L 60
Final L 69
L Blends 79

Initial R 89
Medial R 99
Final R 107
R Blends 117

Initial SH 127
Medial SH 133
Final SH 139

Initial CH 145
Medial CH 151
Final CH 157

Initial J 163
Medial J 169
Final J 175

Introduction

As a speech-language therapist working with elementary students, I'm always looking for motivating ways to help my students improve their speech skills. One day I remembered all the fun I had in elementary school making word catchers (sometimes called "cootie catchers" or "fortune tellers") while I was supposed to be paying attention to the teacher. I decided to try using word catchers with my students to provide extra practice in the correct production of target sounds. My students loved making these word catchers, and their parents reported that students enjoyed using the catchers for practice at home.

Word Catchers for Articulation offers word catchers for the following sounds in initial, medial, and final positions in words:

S	SH
R	CH
L	J

This book also includes word catchers for *S, R,* and *L* blends. Each word catcher provides twelve words with the target sound and eight sentences with at least one occurrence of the target sound. Multiple word catchers are provided for each sound at two levels of difficulty. Level 1 words are mostly short, common words that are easy for students to say and spell. Level 2 words have mostly two or more syllables and they reflect a more sophisticated vocabulary. Younger students should begin working with Level 1 words. Older students may find Level 2 words more comparable to the words they encounter in school.

Using Word Catchers

Select and copy an appropriate word catcher to use with a student. Have the student follow the directions on page 7 to fold and form the word catcher. (For students with motor difficulties, crease the folds ahead of time so that the students only need to position the paper and press down to form their word catchers.)

Before using the word catcher, review the target words in the box at the top of the corresponding word catcher page. Make sure the student understands what each word means. (Asking the student to use the word in a sentence is one way to check for understanding.) Explain any new vocabulary as necessary. Then follow these directions to use the word catcher:

1. The student inserts his thumbs and index fingers below the outside flaps to operate the word catcher. To begin, the student holds the word catcher closed and chooses a picture from one of the outside flaps. The student spells the word below the picture, opening the word catcher for each letter of the word. The example on the next page is for the word *ice*.

Introduction, *continued*

       i   moves thumbs and index fingers apart horizontally
       c   moves thumbs and index fingers apart vertically
       e   moves thumbs and index fingers apart horizontally

2. When the word catcher is opened to spell the last letter, the student chooses one of the words revealed. The student says the word and then spells it, opening the word catcher in opposite directions for each letter.

3. The student chooses another word from the choices revealed. The student says the word, then opens the flap beneath the word and reads aloud the sentence revealed.

4. The student closes the inner flap and closes the word catcher. Then the student repeats steps 1 through 3, selecting different words this time. Repeat the cycle until the student has mastered the words and sentences with 80% accuracy of the target sound.

Here are some additional uses for the word catchers in this book:

- Use the directions for making a word catcher, page 7, as a listening task to help your students practice following oral directions.

- After using a word catcher in therapy, send it home along with a copy of the Homework Helper letter, page 9.

- Have two students use one word catcher together. They can take turns manipulating the word catcher and choosing the words or sentences revealed.

- Have your students color their word catchers and draw pictures of the sentences inside them, such as *A horse goes to bed with shoes on.*

- Copy the blank word catcher on page 8. Choose your own words and sentences.

- A pair of students can play a game with matching word catchers. Student 1 chooses a word or a sentence from inside his word catcher. Student 2 must find the same word or sentence on her word catcher. She must say all the words and sentences she chooses as she tries to find Student 1's word or sentence.

To master a new sound in their speech, students need repeated practice, which is often tedious. Word catchers allow students to have fun while they practice their sounds. You can use the Progress Log, page 10, to keep track of each student's use of specific word catchers. I hope you and your students enjoy these word catchers!

                                                                          Peg Hutson-Nechkash

Making Word Catchers

How to Make a Word Catcher

1. Copy a word catcher from this book. Cut out the word catcher along the dotted lines.
2. Lay the square with the blank side face-up. Fold the paper in half to make a triangle. Make a sharp crease. Open the paper. Fold it in half in the other direction to make a triangle.

 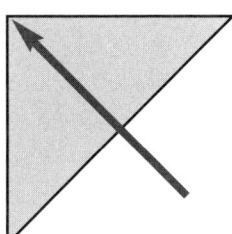 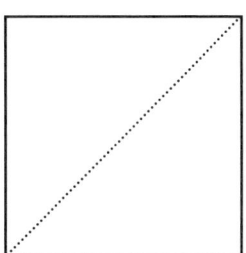 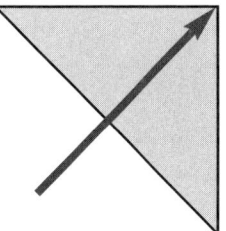 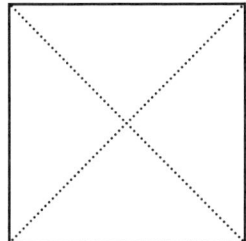

3. Open the paper. Bring each corner to the center of the paper and crease.

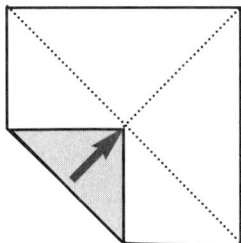 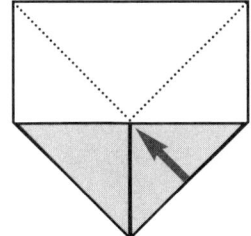 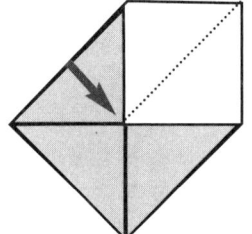 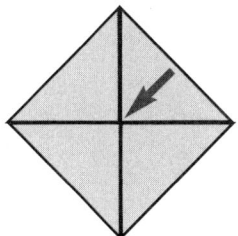

4. Flip the paper over. Bring each corner to the center and crease.

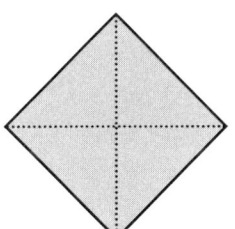 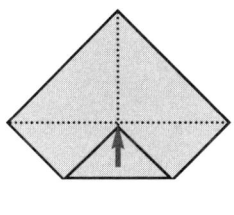 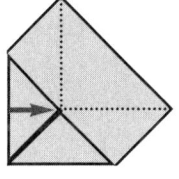 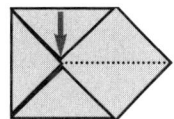 

5. Fold it in half like a book. Open it and fold it in half like a book in the other direction. Open it.

6. Put a thumb or an index finger into each outside flap. Bring the corners together to make the word catcher as shown in the photo.

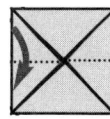

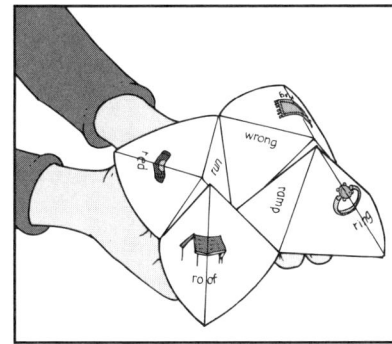

Word Catchers for Articulation
Copyright © 2004 LinguiSystems, Inc.

 # Blank Word Catcher

Add your own words and sentences to this word catcher. Follow the instructions on page 7 to fold it.

Homework Helper Letter

Date _____

Dear Homework Helper,

_____ is currently working on saying the following sound(s) correctly: _____. We have been using word catchers to help practice speaking correctly. These word catchers feature words that include your child's target sound(s).

I am sending a word catcher home with your child. Please help your child use the word catcher to practice words at home. You are an important part of your child's speech training.

Sincerely,

_____
Speech-Language Pathologist

# Progress Log

Student _____

Date	Sound/Position	Word Catcher	Accuracy %

Initial S Level 1	cell	sad	said	saint	say	scents	singe
	cent	saw	sink	sense	sea	someone	surf

cent

cell

You will get a new cell phone.

said

One wall said to the other, "I'll meet you at the corner."

sink

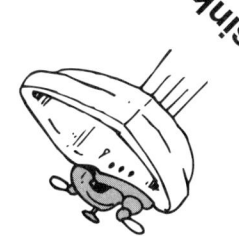

say

You say what you feel.

Saint

A Saint Bernard will lick your face.

surf

Fish don't surf online because they fear the inter-net. (Internet)

scents

A skunk is smart because it makes lots of scents. (sense)

Word Catchers! for Articulation
Copyright © 2004 LinguiSystems, Inc.

saw

singe

Be careful not to singe your hair.

sad

Someone will make you sad.

sea

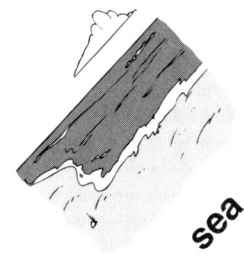

Initial S Level 1	salt	seeds	Sam	seek	sourpuss	sip	soda
	seal	sight	sew	sing	south	sit	sour

seeds

seal

seek

You will seek the seal of approval.

salt

You like salt on your popcorn.

Sam

A seal named Sam will follow you home.

Don't sip Sam's soda.

sour

A cat eating a lemon is a sour puss. (sourpuss)

You will sing a sour note.

Word Catchers! for Articulation™

Copyright © 2004 LinguiSystems, Inc.

sip

sing

sit

Frogs sit on toadstools.

sight

The letter S is never out of SIGHT.

sew

south

Initial S Level 1	set	sack	saved	secret	side	sore	six
	so	safe	scene	solve	soft	soup	sub

soup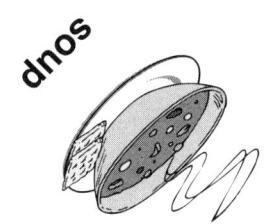

sack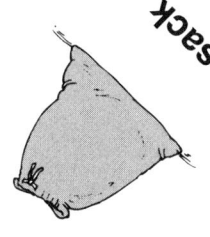

sore You will have a sore toe.

so Your secret is not so safe now.

set You will win a set of Matchbox cars.

soft You like a soft bed.

saved You will be saved from a fall.

side A friend will be on your side.

Copyright © 2004 LinguiSystems, Inc.

sub

solve Solve your problems carefully.

scene Don't make a scene.

six

Initial S Level 1	sob	sail	salve	self	soap	soon	son
	sod	same	satin	sick	sound	sit	

soap

sail

soon Soon you will know the truth.

same A pound of lead and a pound of feathers weigh the same.

salve A salve for pigs is oinkment. (ointment)

sick A sick bird needs to be tweeted. (treated)

son Your aunt's son is your cousin.

self You will read a self-help book.

Word Catchers! for Articulation
Copyright © 2004 LinguiSystems, Inc.

sound

sod Stay off the new sod.

sit You will sit on a satin throne.

sob

Initial S Level 1	safe	silly	scent	some	suit	sunbath	sell
	sank	seen	sings	socks	songs	sword	sis

safe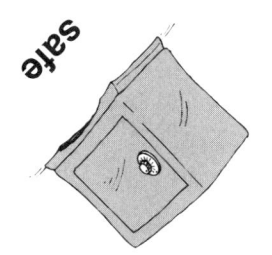

some
Have some fun!

You have seen a ghost.

seen

suit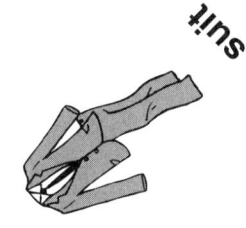

sunbath
You don't need water for a sunbath.

sell
You cannot sell your dirty socks.

Loud socks keep your feet awake.

Your penny sank in a fountain.

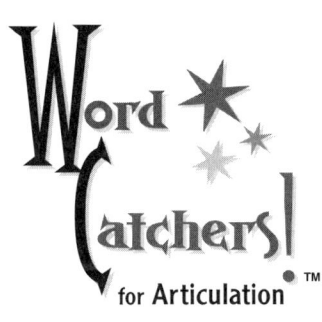

socks

sank

sword

scent
A dog picked up your scent.

Your sis sings silly songs.

sis

songs

Initial S Level 2	circle	saving	senate	signing	someone	seven
	saddle	search	support	soccer	surfboard	syrup

circle

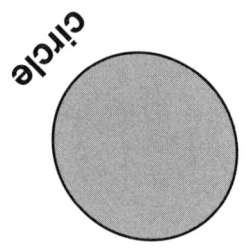

saddle

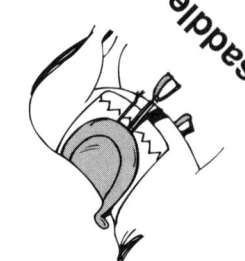

someone
Someone likes you.

support
You support your friends.

soccer
A monster on a soccer team plays ghoulie. (goalie)

senate
You will be in the U.S. Senate.

surfboard
A surfboard is a tongue depressor for a shark.

signing
You will be signing autographs.

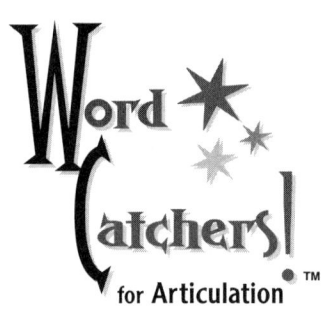

for Articulation™

Copyright © 2004 LinguiSystems, Inc.

syrup

saving
You should be saving more money.

search
You will search for answers.

seven

Initial S Level 2	cycle	sunflower	sandwich	scenic	sub
	sailor	swordfish	soldiers	settle	salty
	sauna	sandwiches	seesaw	sunfish	

sandwich

soldiers

Brave soldiers eat hero sandwiches.

You will take a scenic route.

scenic

seesaw

sunfish

A sunfish is the brightest fish.

sailor

A sailor likes a sub sandwich.

You would like to try a sauna.

Never settle for less than your best.

Word Catchers! for Articulation
Copyright © 2004 LinguiSystems, Inc.

sauna

settle

You will eat a salty sandwich.

Don't cycle in your house.

sunflower

salty

cycle

swordfish

Initial S Level 2	city	cyclone	second	sunglasses	sidewalk	so
	soon	seventy	secret	sideburns	salmon	see
	sadly	sandals	seeing	someone's	sorry	

city

sorry

sunglasses

Your class is so bright, your teacher needs sunglasses.

You will be sorry if you tell someone's secret.

Sideburns make your face hot.

sideburns

sandals

sadly

Sadly, you will have bad luck.

seeing

Soon you will be seeing an old friend.

second

You will be in second place.

After the rain, you will see worms on the sidewalk.

sidewalk

You will find seventy dollars.

seventy

cyclone

salmon

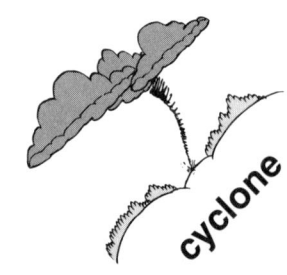

Word Catchers! for Articulation
Copyright © 2004 LinguiSystems, Inc.

Initial S — Level 2

	sock	several	singing	sagebrush	supreme	summer	super
	sofa	socket	surprise	softball	sunburn	Sunday	said

sofa

softball

sunburn — You will get a sunburn.

supreme — You can't play tennis on the Supreme Court.

summer — You will visit the North Pole in the summer.

several — You will surprise several people.

Sunday — Sunday is the best day to go to the beach.

super — You have super powers.

sagebrush

socket — The plug said, "Socket to me." (Sock it)

surprise — You will get a surprise.

singing

Initial S Level 2	sing	certain	sandpaper	seafood	scissors	salad	soda
	silly	cymbals	Saturday	salesman	secret	silver	

soda

certain / **sandpaper**
Are you certain you can keep a secret?
Use sandpaper to write about the beach.

sandpaper

scissors

silver
Silver and gold are your favorite colors.

seafood
Sharks eat a seafood diet.

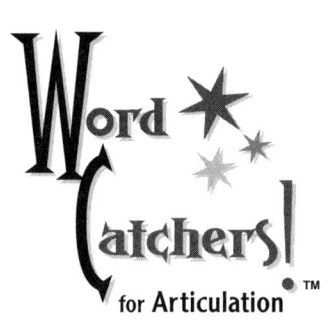

Copyright © 2004 LinguiSystems, Inc.

A shoe salesman went to boot camp.

A silly balloon is an airhead.

salesman

silly

On Saturday you will sing in the shower.

No one will guess your secret.

salad

Saturday

secret

cymbals

Medial S Level 1	messy	baseball	grassy	muscle	nursery	recently	Jason
	icing	bracelet	insect	mussel	outside	whistle	

baseball

messy

You will clean a messy room.

You will watch Jason play baseball.

Jason

bracelet

grassy

You will roll down a grassy hill.

outside

You color outside the lines.

Your arm and the sea each have a muscle. (mussel)

Baby trees go to school at a tree nursery.

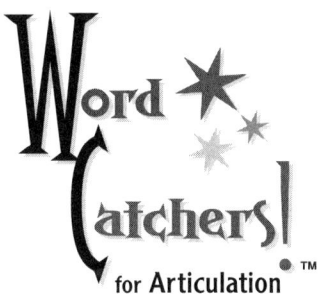

mussel

nursery

A spelling bee is an insect that gets A's.

You have been in trouble recently.

insect

whistle

recently

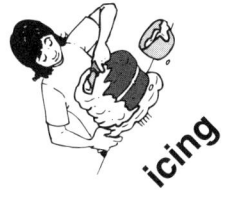

icing

Medial S Level 1	fossil	bicycle	Pacific	listen	teensy	lasso
	castle	grasshopper	missing	pencil	icicle	icy

icicle

icy
Aunty Freeze is an icy aunt. (antifreeze)

missing
Someone is missing you.

pencil

listen
A doctor will listen to your heart.

You will find a fossil near your home.

lasso
You will lasso a grasshopper.

You cannot ride a bicycle on the Pacific Ocean.

Word Catchers! for Articulation

Copyright © 2004 LinguiSystems, Inc.

fossil

Pacific

teensy
A teensy spider will tickle your nose.

castle
You will visit a real castle.

grasshopper

bicycle

Medial S Level 1	bison	braces	disagree	fasten	license	listen	upset
	basin	closer	awesome	fasten	faucet	tracing	gossip

bison

tracing

fasten — Always fasten your seat belt.

closer — Someone wants to be closer to you.

basin

disagree

Fish wash in a river basin.

Don't upset a bison.

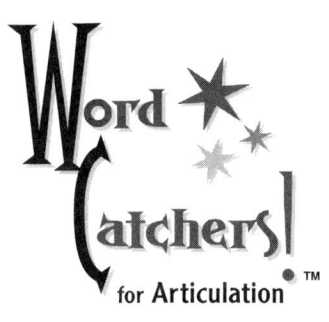

You like to disagree.

Don't listen to gossip.

upset

gossip

license — A screw driver doesn't need a license. (screwdriver)

awesome — You are an awesome artist.

faucet

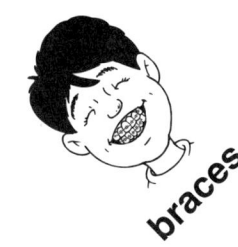

braces

Medial S Level 1	Lisa	hospital	receive	medicine	mousetrap	insect
	essay	blossom	loosen	message	yourself	sassy

insect

essay — You can write an essay with two letters, *S* and *A*.

sassy — Don't be sassy.

hospital

Lisa — Lisa has a message for you.

message — Send a nice message to a friend.

receive — You will receive a reward.

yourself — You will play solitaire by yourself.

loosen — Loosen up! You are too serious.

medicine — A young cat with medicine is a first-aid kit. (kitten)

blossom

mousetrap

Medial S Level 1	answer	concert	dinosaur	glasses	inside	eraser
	beside	decide	massage	himself	kissing	recycle

dinosaur

massage

You will massage someone's foot.

You can't ride on a recycle.

recycle

eraser

inside

You will leave your glasses inside a bus.

concert

You will sing a solo in a concert.

Don't sit beside a dinosaur.

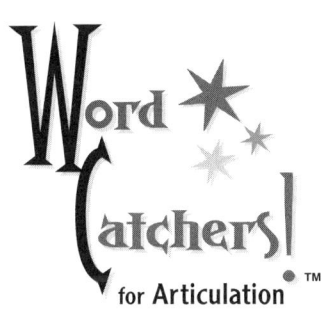

A friend will help himself to your dessert.

beside

himself

You will decide something important soon.

You answer the phone with a pleasant voice.

decide

answer

kissing

glasses

Medial S Level 2	racing chasing dancing exercise glasses officer recipe lesson croissant decision Lifesaver missile possum

possum

officer

At a bakery, a police officer ate a copcake. (cupcake)

dancing

You will go dancing with a possum.

recipe

racing

Don't try racing a missile.

chasing

Some bones were chasing a skull to get ahead. (a head)

You will have a croissant for breakfast.

You will make a wise decision.

decision

exercise

Birds do warm-ups before they exercise. (warm-ups)

You need glasses to read your lesson.

croissant

lesson

Lifesaver

missile

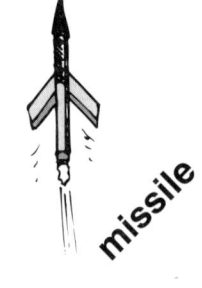

Word Catchers! for Articulation

Copyright © 2004 LinguiSystems, Inc.

Medial S Level 2	juicy	astronaut	cassette	gasoline	passport	tonsils
	oyster	moccasins	eyesight	handsome	sausage	website

oyster

astronaut
An astronaut can't land on a full moon.

Spiders meet at a website.

website

cassette

gasoline
Your car will run out of gasoline.

You have great eyesight.

tonsils
You will have your tonsils taken out.

You will have a juicy sausage for supper.

Copyright © 2004 LinguiSystems, Inc.

eyesight

juicy

moccasins

handsome
You will meet a handsome prince.

You don't need a passport to trip on a rug.

passport

sausage

Medial S Level 2	Alaska	soapsuds	courtesy	greasy	sister
	hassle	classmates	fantasy	outside	insects
	basket	uncertain	mystery	aspirin	bossy

sister

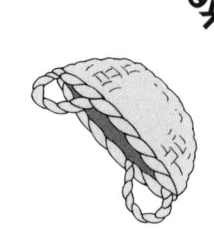

basket

soapsuds

Alaska

Stay away from greasy soapsuds.

You will visit Alaska with your sister.

bossy

courtesy

Do you have a bossy sister?

Your fantasy will come true.

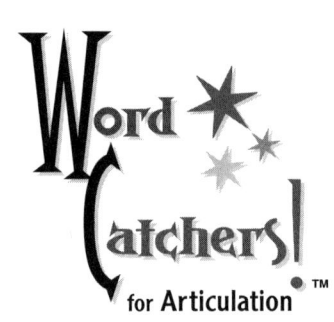

Copyright © 2004 LinguiSystems, Inc.

Show courtesy to your classmates.

Insects will hassle you outside.

fantasy

hassle

Your future career is uncertain.

You will be the first to solve a mystery.

aspirin

uncertain

mystery

insects

Medial S Level 2	dancer	dresser	homesick	motorcycle	passing	places	posse
	ocelot	graceful	listened	disappear	Popsicle	plastic	Tracy

motorcycle

graceful

places

Popsicle

dresser

You are a graceful dancer.

You will visit many places as an adult.

ocelot

You will find a surprise in your dresser.

Does an ocelot talk a lot?

A homesick house went to the doctor.

Your friends are your posse.

Word Catchers! for Articulation
Copyright © 2004 LinguiSystems, Inc.

posse

Your Popsicle will disappear in the sun.

The leftovers listened to plastic rap. (plastic wrap)

homesick

Tracy

disappear

plastic

passing

Final S Level 1	boss	chance	face	Greece	mouse	dice
	bus	cross	floss	guess	peace	plus

bus

plus Learning addition is a real plus!

chance You will have a chance to be on TV.

mouse

floss Did you floss today?

peace Wish for world peace.

Greece You will ride a bus in Greece.

boss You will be the boss of a toy store.

cross The angry puzzle had cross words. (crosswords)

guess Guess what you will dream tonight.

dice

face

Final S Level 1	base	blouse	chase	goose	hiss	price	case
	mess	brace	dance	snakes	lace	dress	

goose

case

mess

dress

You will win a case of soda pop.

Your room is a mess.

chase

lace

A goose will chase you.

You will wear a dress with lace.

You will charge a fair price for your talent.

Snakes study hiss-tory. (history)

price

hiss

blouse

brace

dance

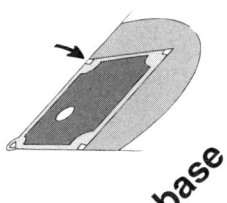
base

Brace yourself for bad news.

You will dance with a goose.

Final S Level 1	ace	Bruce	choice	gloss	less	rice	races
	ice	shoelace	nurse	pulse	miss	this	

Bruce

choice

You will make a good choice.

A nurse will check your pulse.

pulse

ice

miss

You will miss a test.

You will win two races.

Word Catchers! for Articulation™
Copyright © 2004 LinguiSystems, Inc.

less

You will eat less candy this week.

Are you wearing lip gloss?

gloss

races

Your favorite card is the ace of spades.

You will grow an inch this year.

rice

ace

this

shoelace

Final S Level 1	Bess	bounce	dense	grease	house	ice	fence
	once	course	grass	horse	pass	yes	

grass

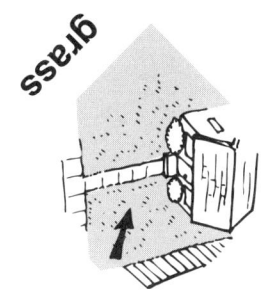

house

bounce

You like to bounce on your bed.

horse

A horse goes to bed with shoes on.

once

fence

A big walnut tree was once a nut like you.

A fence goes around but never moves.

You will walk through a dense fog.

Of course you are smart!

Word Catchers! for Articulation™

Copyright © 2004 LinguiSystems, Inc.

dense

course

grease

yes

Say yes once in a while.

Pass some ice, please.

pass

Bess

Final S Level 1	else	chess	prince	nurse	tense	toss
	nice	class	necklace	purse	worse	vice

purse

nice You look nice today.

vice You will be vice president of your class.

 **chess**

class You will take a chess class.

nurse You will meet a nice nurse.

else What else is wrong?

toss You will toss a salad.

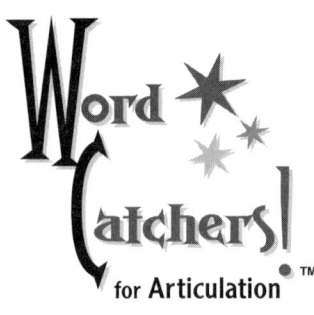

Word Catchers! for Articulation
Copyright © 2004 LinguiSystems, Inc.

necklace

tense You are too tense.

worse Things could be worse.

 **prince**

1

Final S Level 2	bass	glass	kiss	moose	loose	gas	banks
	fuss	juice	kiss	mice	mattress	place	moss

(Final S Level 2: bass, glass, kiss, moose, loose, gas, banks, fuss, juice, mice, mattress, place, moss)

gas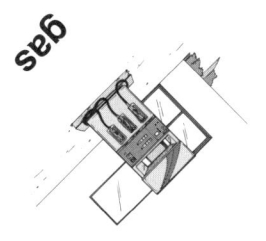

mattress

A moose will jump on your mattress.

bass

Bass keep their money in river banks.

moose

place

You will live in a warm place.

fuss

Don't make a fuss when you make a mistake.

You will have a loose tooth soon.

Mice send each other eek-mail. (e-mail)

loose

mice

Your glass of juice will spill.

You will drink a glass of lemonade.

juice

glass

moss

kiss

Word Catchers for Articulation
Copyright © 2004 LinguiSystems, Inc.

Final S Level 2	cactus	bookcase	chorus	lettuce	promise	thermos	tennis
	bonus	address	famous	points	sickness	witness	

cactus

bookcase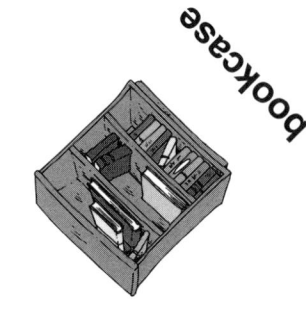

witness — You will be a witness in a court trial.

promise — You can break a promise without touching it.

chorus — A cow chorus sang in beef-flat. (*B*-flat)

address — You will change your address.

famous — You will be very famous.

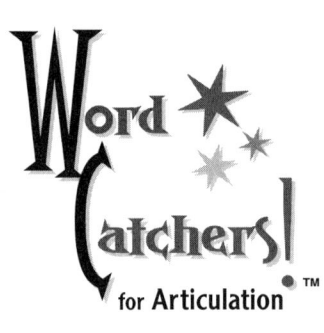

points — You will earn bonus points in a contest.

bonus

thermos

tennis — You will raise a racket in a tennis game.

sickness — Sitting on a cactus could cause a sickness.

lettuce

Final S Level 2	minus	baldness	purpose	porpoise	confess	advice
	erase	fireplace	octopus	progress	palace	notice

octopus

erase

purpose

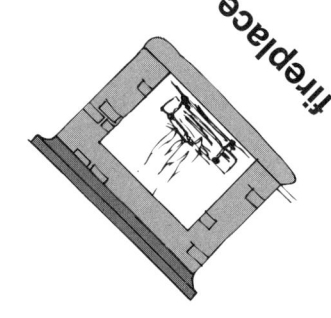

fireplace

You will erase the wrong answer.

A porpoise will splash you on purpose.

progress

minus

You will make great progress in math.

Your jacket is minus one button.

No one will notice your haircut.

You will confess to telling a secret.

Word Catchers! for Articulation

Copyright © 2004 LinguiSystems, Inc.

notice

confess

Good advice is hard to find.

Losing hair causes baldness.

advice

porpoise

baldness

palace

Final S Level 2	focus	curious	doghouse	impress	Paris
	circus	dentist's	paradise	walrus	tricks
	compass	caboose	lioness	office	Lois

walrus

doghouse

focus You need to focus on your homework.

curious You are curious about the future.

lioness A lioness will escape from the circus.

A dentist's office is a filling station.

paradise You will visit a tropical paradise.

You will impress your friends with yo-yo tricks.

Word Catchers! for Articulation
Copyright © 2004 LinguiSystems, Inc.

office

impress

Paris You will live in a doghouse in Paris.

Superman's favorite street is Lois Lane.

compass

Lois

caboose

Final S — Level 2 — 5

apes	dollhouse	nervous	lighthouse	tortoise	police
virus	jealous	replace	business	makes	walrus
class	kindness	terrace	necklace		

tortoise

police

virus

Your computer will get sick with a virus.

Someone is jealous of you.

jealous

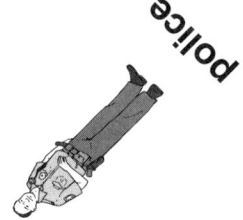

lighthouse

replace

You will visit a lighthouse.

A walrus will give you a necklace.

No one could replace you.

A lion in your class makes you nervous.

Word Catchers! for Articulation
Copyright © 2004 LinguiSystems, Inc.

walrus

nervous

Four apes had a monkey business.

Your kindness will be rewarded.

terrace

business

kindness

dollhouse

S Blends Level 1	slow	slugs	school	snail	smart	stay
	spot	smack	starfish	snake	smarty	swam
	slide	scare	spider	spray	smash	

slide

scare

A witch wears scare spray on her hair. (hair spray)

Smart kids wear smarty-pants.

smart

smash

spot

Spot is not a good name for a zebra.

A prison for slow slugs is a snail jail.

snake

A tattlesnake will tell on you. (rattlesnake)

You smack your lips in class.

slow

smack

Cows stay in moo-tels. (motels)

A starfish swam to the movies.

spider

stay

swam

school

S Blends Level 1	skis	slope	sloppy	smell	spend	stays	string	snow
	sled	smile	skates	snail	stamp	steam	swell	slip

skates

smell

Nice perfume is a swell smell.

A tired steam iron ran out of steam.

steam

sled

slip

Your skis will slip on the slope.

You will walk a mile in the snow.

stamp

A stamp travels the world but stays in a corner.

You will spend all of your allowance.

snow

spend

Pigs keep their data on sloppy disks. (floppy disks)

You will plant string beans in a garden.

sloppy

string

snail

smile

S Blends Level 1	desk	first	moist	most	postage	talks	toast	test
	last	ghost	paste	nest	roast	task	waste	

paste

ghost

roast

moist

You will eat roast beef on toast.

A letter was moist because it had postage dew. (due)

last

first

You will be the last one to finish lunch.

Turtles were the first to have mobile homes.

Eye doctors and teachers both test pupils.

Don't waste time.

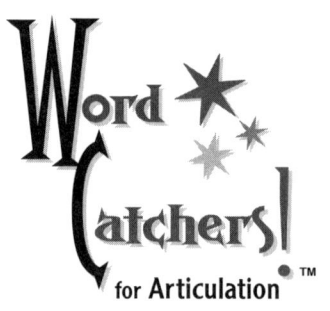

Copyright © 2004 LinguiSystems, Inc.

test

waste

The animal that talks the most is a yak.

You will finish a task quickly.

desk

most

task

nest

4

S Blends Level 1	vest	beast	mask	chest	post	twist	fast
	west	blast	most	crossed	east	wrist	

chest

wrist

twist

crossed

You will twist some taffy.

You crossed a street without looking.

east

beast

You will travel from east to west.

You will do the twist with a beast.

A fast duck is a quick quack.

A quick noise is a fast blast.

fast

blast

vest

west

post

mask

You will ride a horse in the West.

The two words with the most letters are *post office*.

Word Catchers for Articulation
Copyright © 2004 LinguiSystems, Inc.

S Blends Level 1	disk	elephants	list	locks	plates	pants	ticks	pest
	eats	trunks	lots	notes	sleeps	ships	wants	fox

ticks — A watchdog has lots of ticks.

locks — All the doors in the Three Bears' house have Goldi-locks. (gold locks)

plates — A car eats off of license plates.

trunks — Elephants, trees, and cars all have trunks.

ships — Never use the sink on ships.

notes — You pass notes in class.

sleeps — A gorilla sleeps anyplace he wants.

pest — Don't be a pest.

fox

pants

list

disk

★1★

S Blends Level 2	swap	steed	scarecrow	steal	sleeve	swimsuit	sloth
	smog	skinny	spaghetti	space	speed	spotless	stain

scarecrow

space

speed

sloth

A sick astronaut takes a space capsule.

A fast horse is a speed steed.

sleeve

steal

You have a stain on your sleeve.

You will steal a base in baseball.

Someone wants to swap places with you.

Fix broken spaghetti with tomato paste.

Copyright © 2004 LinguiSystems, Inc.

swap

skinny

spotless

spaghetti

A skinny scarecrow tells corny jokes.

After his bath, the leopard was spotless.

smog

swimsuit

S Blends Level 2	spotlight	scarf	sleeping	sticky	stinking	skunks
	scholarship	study	sweater	stirrup	skeleton	sweet
	swamped	snore	students	scholar		

sweater
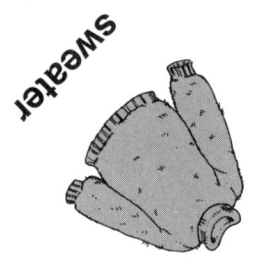

skunks

Smart skunks wear stinking caps. (thinking caps)

students

Students travel on a scholar-ship. (scholarship)

scarf

sweet

Someone thinks you are sweet.

sticky

Working in a glue factory is sticky work.

snore

If bananas snore, they wake up the whole bunch.

Word Catchers! for Articulation

Copyright © 2004 LinguiSystems, Inc.

A bull dozer is a sleeping bull. (bulldozer)

sleeping

stirrup

Horses eat maple stirrup on pancakes. (syrup)

Frogs study hard when they are swamped.

swamped

spotlight

skeleton

S Blends Level 2

stick	smellers	spring	swallows	strong	swine
spill	skunks	stakes	sweepstakes	sweep	swing
snail	sports	storm	sneakers		

sneakers

sports

spring

Bedbugs get married in the spring.

smellers
Skunks read best smellers. (best sellers)

swallowed

A cat that swallows wool has mittens. (kittens)

A broom won the sweep-stakes. (sweepstakes)

swine

Pigs in trouble call swine-one-one. (911)

A snail is strong because it carries its house.

strong

sweep

spill
You will spill your milk at lunch.

stick
A magician's wand is a trick stick.

swing

storm

4

S Blends Level 2	ax	snowball	gates	maps	goats	tapes
	pox	snowflakes	bumps	pets	pants	stick
	lips	brakes	kites	ants		

gates

kites

pox

tapes

A sick chicken had people pox.

Someone will stick tapes on your pants.

snowflakes

goats

Snowflakes dance at the snowball. (snow ball)

Treat baby goats like kids.

You will get goose bumps.

Faces and gardens have two lips. (tulips)

lips

ants

You will have ants for pets.

A mechanic was fired for taking too many brakes. (breaks)

bumps

brakes

ax

maps

5

S Blends Level 2	box	boats	cornstalks	ropes	cheeks	peanuts	tracks	fast
	lots	boots	mailbox	taste	worst	pierced	what's	fist

mailbox

lots

tracks

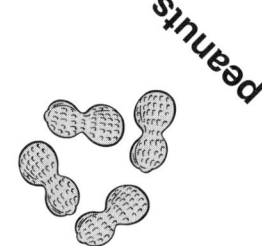

peanuts

Boats park in yacht lots.

Someone is following in your tracks.

worst

cheeks

What's the worst that could happen?

Someone will pinch your cheeks.

Some cornstalks had their ears pierced.

Hands eat at a fist-food restaurant. (fast-food)

Word Catchers! for Articulation™

Copyright © 2004 LinguiSystems, Inc.

pierced

fist

taste

box

boots

ropes

A box has two sides, inside and outside.

The boots decided to go on foot.

Initial L Level 1	lie	lake	lamp	lemon	let's	like	lost
	leg	lamb	late	longer	light	look	lot

leg

lemon

lot

You have a lot of friends.

like

You like to look in the mirror.

let's

A lamp said, "Let's go out tonight."

lamb

A sick lamb took a lambulance to the hospital. (ambulance)

A horse that stays up late is a night mare. (nightmare)

Light can go through water without getting wet.

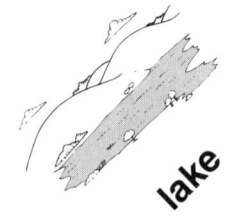

late

lamp

lost

A dog that is no longer lost is a found hound.

Whales lie on a water bed.

light

lie

lake

Word Catchers! for Articulation
Copyright © 2004 LinguiSystems, Inc.

Initial L Level 1	lie	large	ladder	long	loud	luck	legs
	lion	live	ladybug	loses	loves	lucky	

lion

large
A large ladybug will bring you good luck.

live
City ducks live in pondos. (condos)

ladder

loves
You know someone who loves broccoli.

Loud pants keep your legs from falling asleep.

long
The best way to call a lion is long distance.

Elephants lie in the middle of the road to trip ants.

loud

A refrigerator loses its cool when you unplug it.

The best key to have is luck-key. (lucky)

lie

lucky

loses

luck

ladybug

Initial L Level 1	lady	later	looking	letter	leaves	loose	lime
	land	laugh	leopard	lunch	living	limit	love

lady

A lady is looking for you.

limit

There is no limit to what you can do.

land

You will land on Mars someday.

looking

You will be looking for your lunch.

loose

A loose leopard will follow you home.

letter

A snake signs a letter with love and hisses. (kisses)

laugh

later

A baseball glove said to a baseball, "Catch you later."

living

A ghost doesn't need a living room.

leopard

Initial L Level 1	lie	leaky	learned	list	lettuce	light	lobster	lose
	lap	lying	lesson	lamp	lumber	little	lonely	left

left

little

lap

list

A little monster ate his lamp for a light dinner.

You lose your lap when you stand up.

lesson

leaky

You have learned your lesson.

You run faster than a leaky faucet.

You have told a little white lie.

Lumber is always bored. (board)

lie

lumber

Never believe anyone who is lying in bed.

Bananas aren't lonely. They hang out in bunches.

lying

lonely

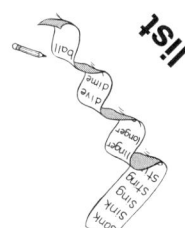

lobster

lettuce

5

Initial L Level 1	lab	lunch	last	leaving	lines	license	life
	laptop	learn	lazy	language	long	lizard	lace

lizard

last

Elephants are the last ones to pack their trunks.

lab

The scientist's computer was a lab-top. (laptop)

lace

language

You will learn a new language.

leaving

You will be leaving on a jet plane.

Word Catchers! for Articulation

Copyright © 2004 LinguiSystems, Inc.

Your car eats off a license plate.

A lazy baby kangaroo is a pouch potato. (couch potato)

license

lazy

A king drew straight lines because he was a ruler.

You will have a long and happy life.

lines

life

lunch

learn

Initial L Level 2	lice lawsuit loaf luggage loser limbo lotion leap
	like lawyer lily lemonade layer llama leader

lily

leap — The best year for kangaroos is leap year.

limbo — Never limbo under an electric fence.

lotion

lice — Insects put lice cubes in their lemonade. (ice cubes)

A smaller beach is a shore loser. (sore loser)

layer — Chickens like to eat layer cakes.

loaf — Bread makers loaf on their day off.

loser

luggage

lawsuit — A lawyer doesn't wear a lawsuit.

You are a leader in your class.

leader

llama

Word Catchers! for Articulation
Copyright © 2004 LinguiSystems, Inc.

Initial L Level 2

Initial L Level 2	leg	lagoon	listen	library	lamp
	lava	laundry	larva	lipstick	lifts
	limp	lantern	lower	locket	love

lipstick

love

Ghosts fall in love at first fright. (first sight)

larva

A moth has a larva lamp in its room. (lava lamp)

locket

listen

Listen to sheet music in bed.

lower

Your voice is getting lower.

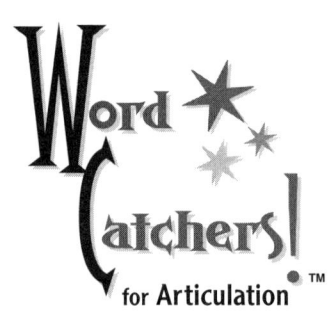

The bird that lifts the most is a crane.

A chimpanzee with a broken leg has a chimp limp.

lifts

limp

Birds go to the library to find bookworms.

You will swim in a lagoon with a baboon.

lantern

library

lagoon

laundry

Initial L Level 2	lips	laziest	litter	lifeguard	lousy	liquid	Luis
	lava	Liberty	lasso	longest	love	locker	like

Luis

lousy

You don't need a lousy grade.

lips

The flowers on every face are tu-lips. (two lips)

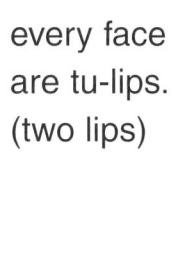

locker

Liberty

You will visit the Statue of Liberty.

lava

A volcano asked, "Do you lava me like I lava you?" (love)

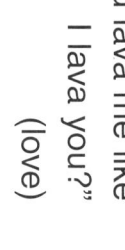

A cat was arrested for kitty litter.

Equator is the longest word because it circles the globe.

litter

Your favorite liquid is chocolate milk.

The laziest mountain is Mt. Ever-rest. (Everest)

longest

lasso

liquid

laziest

lifeguard

Initial L — Level 2

	lane	lawn mower	lead	leagues	licked
	lark	lighthouse	live	locate	least
	law	lemonade	leash	leisure	lover's

lemonade

licked
In a candy fight, the suckers were licked.

law
You obey the law.

lark

cheep cheep

locate
You will locate a treasure map.

least
The house that weighs the least is a lighthouse.

lead
A heavy pencil is full of lead.

leisure
Bees have no leisure time because they are always buzzy. (busy)

leagues
You will play in the big leagues.

lane
You will live on Lover's Lane.

lawn mower

leash

Initial L Level 2	laid	latch	lumps	lasagna	link	leather	lock
	limo	leech	lunar	linebacker	load	lecture	

limo

laid
A sick housecleaner is a laid-up maid.

lunar
You will watch a lunar eclipse.

lock

link
There is a link between studying and good grades.

A leech will latch onto you.

lumps
Marbles in mashed potatoes cause lumps.

A linebacker who adds numbers is a math-lete. (athlete)

latch

linebacker

leather

lecture
A lecture by the ocean is a beach speech.

load
Sit down! Take a load off your feet.

lasagna

Word Catchers! for Articulation™
Copyright © 2004 LinguiSystems, Inc.

Medial L Level 1	gold	police	tadpoles	salad	mild
	cold	child	watercolors	violin	silly
	poles	jelly	volcano	eleven	colors

salad

jelly

police

You will thank a police officer.

poles

Three famous poles are: North Pole, South Pole, and tadpoles.

colors

You need watercolors to paint the ocean.

volcano

You will watch a volcano blow its top.

cold

When you catch a cold, you don't feel so hot.

You like to act silly.

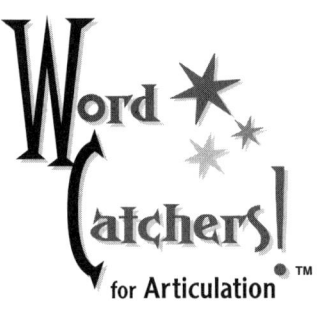

silly

child

A gentle baby is a mild child.

Little astronauts get gold stars on their papers.

violin

gold

eleven

Medial L Level 1	old	belt	bowling	celery	ruler	chili
	cold	bills	animals	walrus	smells	alley
	talk	pilot	family	chilly		

pilot

talk

You can talk to animals.

alley

Alley cats like to go bowling.

ruler

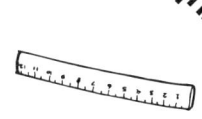

belt

Always buckle your seat belt.

bowling

You will go bowling with a walrus.

A cold hot dog is a chilly dog. (chili dog)

A sad duck family has lots of bills.

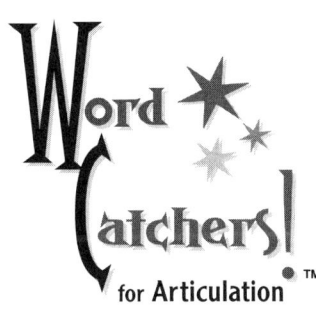

Copyright © 2004 LinguiSystems, Inc.

chilly

family

An elephant's toothbrush smells like peanuts.

You will find an old map.

walrus

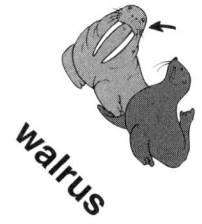

old

smells

celery

Medial L Level 1	gulp	salsa	balloon	collar	follow	pillow	silly
	wolf	holly	noodles	elbow	quickly	sailor	

balloon

salsa

Salsa stays hot in a refrigerator.

A silly gardener gave a thirsty tree a root beer.

silly

elbow

noodles

Use tomato paste to mend broken spaghetti noodles.

Movie stars build their houses with holly-wood. (Hollywood)

holly

You will follow your dreams.

Never argue with a wolf.

follow

wolf

A sailor sends a letter through sea-mail. (e-mail)

A fish that drinks quickly is a gulp-y. (guppy)

sailor

gulp

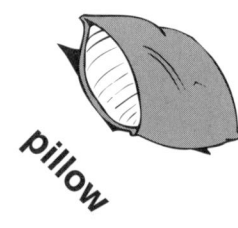

pillow

collar

Medial L Level 1	polar	catalog	deliver	really	skeleton	mellow	roller
	tulips	ceiling	dollar	totally	formula	fellow	melon

dollar

fellow

polar

tulips

A calm man is a mellow fellow.

A polar bear has great ice-sight. (eyesight)

really

catalog

A really cool frog is toad-ally awesome. (totally)

Cats order from a cat-alog. (catalog)

You will create a magic formula.

Use a skeleton key to get into a haunted house.

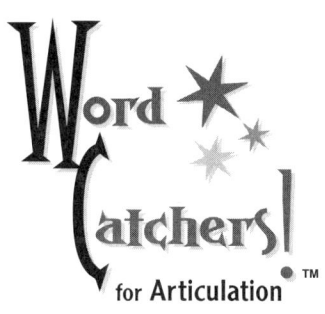

formula

skeleton

Someone will deliver tulips to you.

A skater can shave with a roller-blade.

melon

deliver

roller

ceiling

Medial L Level 1	tales	along	buffalo	July	gorilla	related	yellow	milk
	told	cooler	dollars	relay	million	spelling	ruler	

milk

spelling

A spelling bee won't sting you.

relay

You will run a relay race with a gorilla.

yellow

July

You will milk a cow in July.

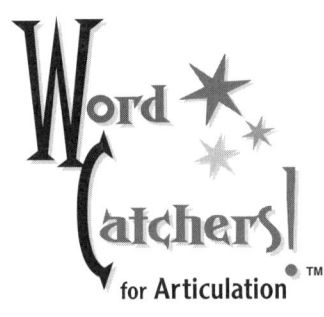

related

You are related to a buffalo.

An awesome queen is a cooler ruler.

You will win a million dollars.

million

along

A fence runs along a yard without moving.

told

A giant told tall tales in school.

cooler

gorilla

buffalo

Medial L Level 2	meals olive ocelot	bachelor telephone swallowed	omelet squeals walnuts	jellyfish calendar umbrella	believe bolted wheels

ocelot

calendar

A bachelor bought a calendar to get dates.

You are nuts about walnuts.

walnuts

umbrella

bolted

A bolted door keeps nuts out.

believe

A shark's favorite sandwich is peanut butter and jellyfish.

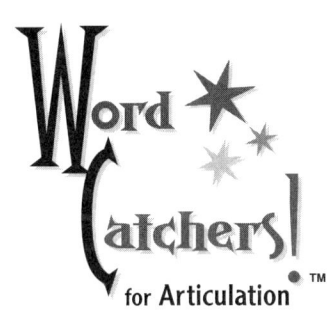

You don't believe in gravity.

An omelet your mom makes is a momelet. (omelet)

jellyfish

A dog that swallowed a watch had lots of ticks.

Pigs that drive trucks are squeals on wheels. (meals on wheels)

omelet

telephone

swallowed

wheels

olive

Word Catchers for Articulation

Medial L Level 2	lily	volleyball	elderly	holiday	helicopter	pelican
	old	celebrated	antlers	alligator	fabulous	stroller
	valley	dandelion	follow	piccolo	snorkeling	

stroller

fabulous

F on a report card does not mean "fabulous."

An alligator will follow you to school.

alligator

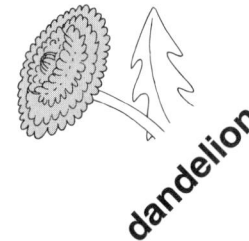

helicopter

celebrated

A holiday will be celebrated in your honor.

piccolo

A musical pickle is a piccolo.

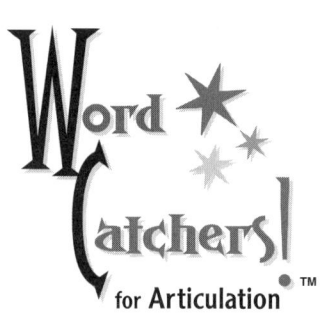

Copyright © 2004 LinguiSystems, Inc.

Your favorite flower is a lily of the volleyball. (valley)

Too much moose in your hair causes antlers. (mousse)

volleyball

antlers

Elderly eggs live in an old-yolks home. (old-folks)

Don't snore when you are snorkeling.

elderly

snorkeling

pelican

dandelion

Medial L Level 2	aliens	bologna	talent	highlighter	dolphin	island	violets
	ballots	violence	trailer	pointless	palace	wallet	

island

wallet

Don't lose your wallet.

bologna

The bologna said, "It's nice to meat you." (meet)

palace

talent

You have hidden talent.

pointless

A broken pencil is pointless.

highlighter

When you write on a plane, use a highlighter.

Dangerous flowers are violence. (violets)

violence

trailer

ballots

A bag that carries ballots is a vote tote.

You will live in a palace with aliens.

aliens

dolphin

Medial L — Level 2

solar	athlete	belong	silence	peelings	gallon	alarm
solo	ballet	feelings	tailor	mallard	salami	alike

gallon

tailor

athlete

salami

A tailor is a sew pro.

You will be a great athlete.

ballet

silence

You belong in a ballet class.

One word can break a silence.

You and a wise owl are alike.

You will sing a solo.

alike

solo

An orange said, "You hurt my peelings." (feelings)

You are full of solar energy.

mallard

solar

peelings

alarm

Final L Level 1	all	bull	hole	smell	style	whale	will
	ball	full	roll	smile	table	wool	well

ball

hole

table

A table has four legs but can't walk.

full

A full moon isn't hungry.

all

Have you done all of your homework?

bull

A bulldozer is a sleeping bull.

A cooked roll is a done bun.

Your smile will always be in style.

Word Catchers! for Articulation
Copyright © 2004 LinguiSystems, Inc.

roll

style

smile

wool

Send a sick sheep a get-wool-soon card.
(get-well-soon)

smell

Noses can run and feet can smell.

whale

2

Final L Level 1	doll	call	jewel	feel	small	wall
	bell	chill	apple	hall	wheel	will
	bill	dial	people	owl		

bell

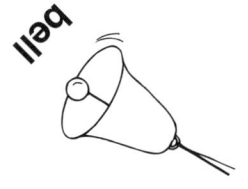

apple

City worms live in the Big Apple.

bill

When a duck buys lipstick, she puts it on her bill.

doll

jewel

You will find a jewel in the hall.

wall

A wall told another wall, "Meet you at the corner."

You feel great today!

Small people call each other on micro-phones. (microphones)

feel

dial

A tree with an emergency will dial pine-one-one. (911)

Spiders give you a chill.

small

wheel

chill

owl

Final L — Level 1

	jail	crawl	mail	pupil	nail	swell	smell	pull
	call	cruel	mall	school	bowl	towel	snail	tall

bowl

cruel
It's cruel to pull corn by the ear.

tall
Tall giraffes go to high school.

nail

pupil
An eye and a school each have a pupil.

Slow slugs go to a snail jail.

call
If you stub your foot, don't call a toe truck. (tow truck)

A day of shopping is a mall crawl.

Word Catchers! for Articulation
Copyright © 2004 LinguiSystems, Inc.

jail

mail
Jellyfish send sea-mail. (e-mail)

A nice perfume is a swell smell.

crawl

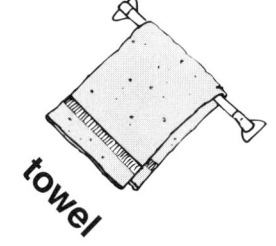

towel

swell

snail

Final L Level 1	all	carpool	well	stool	shell	mill
	oil	needle	pole	pool	spill	will
	girl	treadmill	stale	seal	pal	

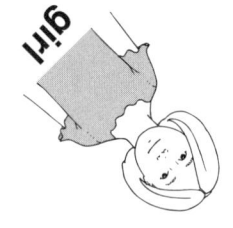
girl

stale

Your lunch sandwich will be stale.

mill

A needle works out on a thread-mill. (treadmill)

seal

pal

A pig wants you for a pen pal.

A pool with no water is a carpool.

pole

You will visit the South Pole.

You will spill your milk today.

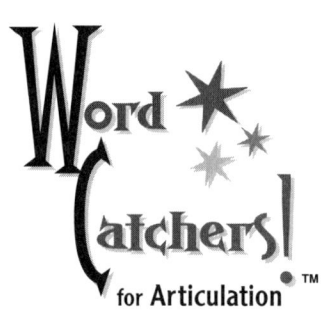
Copyright © 2004 LinguiSystems, Inc.

pool

A needle has an eye but can't see at all.

You will own an oil well.

spill

needle

oil

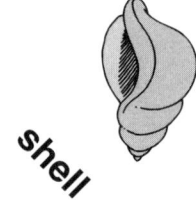
shell

stool

| Final L | well | fall | pencil | shall | tale | trail | turtle | will |
| Level 1 | eel | tell | school | spell | mule | while | camel | |

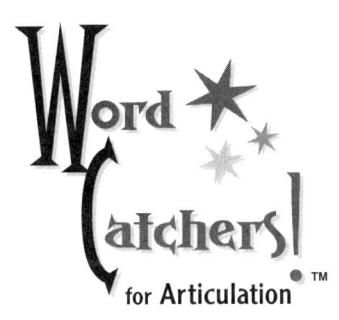

Word Catchers! for Articulation™
Copyright © 2004 LinguiSystems, Inc.

camel

eel

shall — You shall wash your own clothes from now on.

tell — A watchdog can tell time.

spell — You can spell tricky words well.

tale — Your favorite fairy tale is Sleeping Beauty.

while — You have fun while you are in school.

fall — You will fall in love someday.

mule — Donkey students ride a mule bus. (school bus)

trail — You will ride a camel on a trail.

turtle

pencil

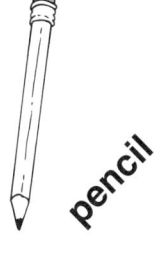

Final L Level 2	ball	eagle	tonsil	grill	noodle	eyeball	foul	will
	ill	scale	jingle	pale	pickle	snowball	pail	I'll
	dill	carol	jungle	vowel	poodle	football		

grill

scale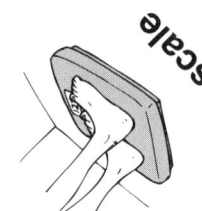

vowel

tonsil

Bad letters use vowel language. (foul language)

A doctor told a tonsil, "I'll take you out tonight."

eagle

poodle

You will soar like an eagle.

Dogs like chicken-poodle soup. (chicken-noodle)

A sick pickle is an ill dill.

Glasses dance at the eye ball. (eyeball)

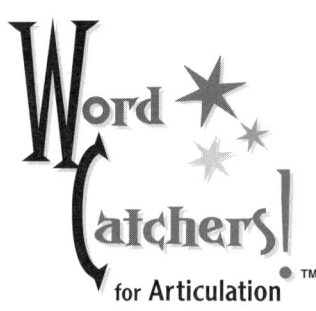

Copyright © 2004 LinguiSystems, Inc.

dill

eyeball

A bucket said, "You look pail today." (pale)

Tarzan's favorite carol is "Jungle Bells." ("Jingle Bells")

pail

carol

snowball

football

Final L — Level 2

ill	candle	crocodile	musical	tadpole	school
will	cereal	football	noodle	waterfall	sundial
bowl	channel	muscle	pigtail		

school

cereal

You will play football in the cereal bowl.

channel

Your TV can't swim the English Channel.

muscle

waterfall

Don't throw water out the window to see a waterfall.

ill

A sick crocodile is said, "I will be going out tonight." (alligator)

Word Catchers! for Articulation™

Copyright © 2004 LinguiSystems, Inc.

musical

You have musical talent.

candle

A candle

pigtail

sundial

Tune into the sun with a sundial.

noodle

Noodle soup is good for the brain.

tadpole

Final L Level 2	will	windmill	tattle	oatmeal	ankle	nail
	tell	journal	animal	parasol	bowl	drill
	file	baseball	marble	snuggle		

parasol

journal

Write in your journal every day.

You can file a nail under the letter *N*.

file

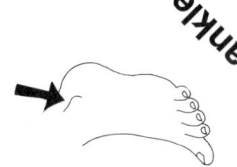

ankle

drill

A group of dentists is a drill team.

Marble cake is as hard as a rock.

tattle

A tattlesnake will tell on you. (rattlesnake)

You will win a bowl of oatmeal.

Word Catchers! for Articulation

Copyright © 2004 LinguiSystems, Inc.

marble

oatmeal

You like animal crackers in a box.

Don't snuggle with a porcupine.

windmill

animal

snuggle

baseball

Final L Level 2	bubble	coral	basketball	circle	middle	trouble	whole	will
	bottle	maple	bicycle	medal	snorkle	travel	school	well

basketball

bubble

A bubble is light but can't be lifted.

whole

Your whole future is in your hands.

circle

bottle

A bottle has a neck but no head.

It is smart to stay out of trouble.

maple

You like maple syrup over ice cream.

You will do well in middle school.

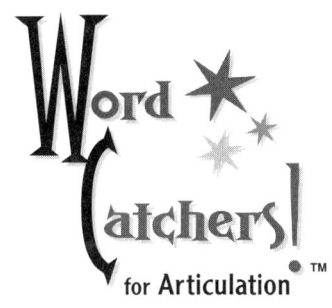
Copyright © 2004 LinguiSystems, Inc.

trouble

middle

coral

You will snorkle near a coral reef.

You will travel to the Arctic Circle.

travel

bicycle

medal

Final L Level 2	April	buttonhole	reptile	carnival	earful	sail
	scowl	triangle	vessel	cheerful	missile	will
	wheel	vegetable	cattle	pretzel	battle	

April

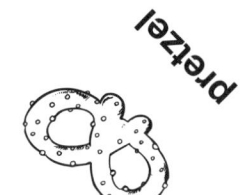

pretzel

scowl

Someone will scowl at you today.

cattle

A bullfight is a cattle battle.

missile

An astronaut stubbed his missile toe. (mistletoe)

vessel

You can't sail on a blood vessel.

You will ride a Ferris wheel at a carnival.

You will dance with a reptile.

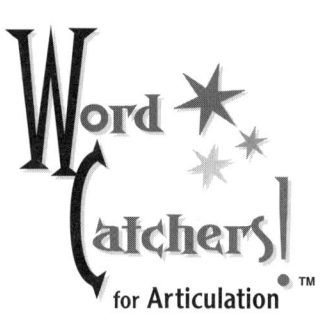

for Articulation

Copyright © 2004 LinguiSystems, Inc.

carnival

reptile

earful

Good news is a cheerful earful.

vegetable

A jellybean is not a vegetable.

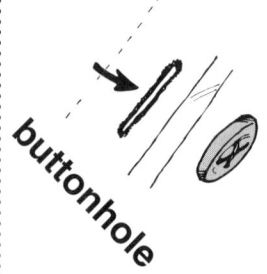

buttonhole

triangle

L Blends Level 1	clue	black	flags	blubber	plate	sled
	flop	close	glad	clouds	sleek	glue

black

flop

Popcorn that doesn't pop is flop corn.

A thin duck's bill is a sleek beak.

sleek

flags

clue

A group of detectives is a clue crew.

close

You will have many close friends.

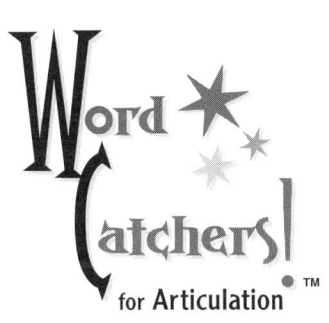

Whales chew blubber gum. (bubblegum)

Rain clouds wear thunderwear. (underwear)

blubber

A dog's favorite food is anything on your plate.

A high school senior is a glad grad.

clouds

plate

glad

sled

glue

Word Catchers for Articulation
Copyright © 2004 LinguiSystems, Inc.

L Blends Level 1	flat	blanket	flake	floppy	place	plow	slide	slow
	slob	sloppy	floor	gloves	plant	sleep	blocks	

blocks

place

You will visit a new place.

slob

A slob saves data on a sloppy disk. (floppy disk)

gloves

blanket

A horse got a blanket because he was a little colt. (cold)

Keep your feet flat on the floor.

Copyright © 2004 LinguiSystems, Inc.

plow

You will plow a path through snow.

A snow shovel is a flake rake.

flat

plant

slow

You like slow music best.

sleep

You sleep like a baby.

flake

slide

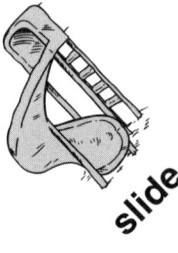

L Blends Level 1	blab	clock	flower	club	cluck	glass	slug
	fly	clover	planet	plan	flame	slimy	split

flower

blab

A taxi that talks is a blab cab.

A slimy slug will cross your path.

slimy

clover

club

A bathtub joined the tub club.

Chickens wake up at seven o'cluck. (o'clock)

split

You will split a banana with a friend.

You will live on another planet.

Copyright © 2004 LinguiSystems, Inc.

cluck

planet

A firefighter visited the Hall of Flame. (Hall of Fame)

Plan to succeed in all you do.

flame

plan

glass

fly

L Blends Level 1	plus	splash	flip-flops	globe	plate	flies
	blew	blouse	sleeve	blame	climb	slice

sleeve

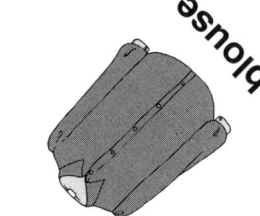

blouse

splash

blame

You will make a big splash.

Don't blame anyone for your mistakes.

plus

slice

Learning to add is a real plus.

Don't eat flies on a slice of pizza.

Word Catchers! for Articulation

Copyright © 2004 LinguiSystems, Inc.

You will climb hills all over the globe.

A chimney got angry and blew its stack.

climb

blew

A garbage truck has four wheels and flies.

You will get a new pair of flip-flops.

plate

flies

flip-flops

globe

L Blends Level 1	flea	planet	played	playpen	Pluto	plane	slop	plum
	play	clothes	floor	flashlight	glove	blond	flap	

flashlight

glove

plum

play

A mitten told a thumb, "I glove you." (love)

Babies write with a play pen. (playpen)

blond

flea

A bald eagle bought a blond wig.

A pig played short-slop on the baseball team. (shortstop)

Bugs send flea mail. (e-mail)

You will visit the planet Pluto.

slop

Pluto

Your ears flap in the wind.

Don't throw your clothes on the floor.

flap

clothes

plane

floor

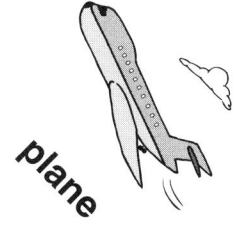
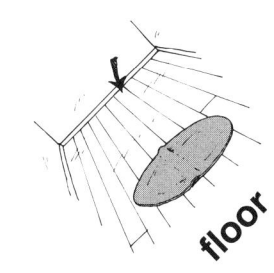

L Blends Level 2	play	blizzard	flute	slumber	pliers	slipped	sloth
	plot	climate	glider	plastic	sleep	slippers	glum

glider

plot

You can find a plot in a garden and a story.

slipped

A computer with a slipped disk stayed in bed.

slippers

blizzard

Toto was cold in the *Blizzard of Oz*. (*Wizard of Oz*)

You will live in a cold climate.

Copyright © 2004 LinguiSystems, Inc.

plastic

You will play a plastic flute.

Multi-pliers are good at math. (multipliers)

climate

A slumber-jack cuts wood in his sleep. (lumberjack)

An unhappy friend is a glum chum.

pliers

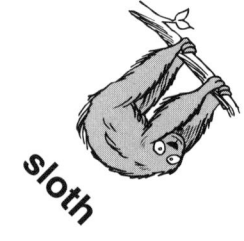

sloth

slumber

glum

flute

L Blends Level 2	clap	sliver	clinic	flamingo	slide	blender	florist	slick
	clip	blood	flower	playpen	sling	clowns	slope	

flamingo

clowns

Sharks don't eat clowns because they taste funny.

If you fall into a blender, you will be mixed up.

blender

clip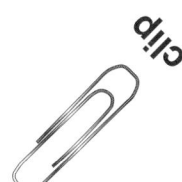

sliver

You will get a sliver of cake on your birthday.

You will slide on a slick slope.

florist

A flower shop on fire is a florist fire. (forest fire)

A flamingo will clap for you.

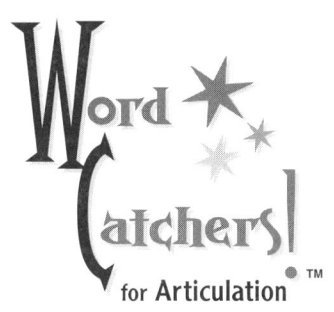

Copyright © 2004 LinguiSystems, Inc.

slick

A vampire works at a blood bank.

A computer with a virus went to a clinic.

clap

playpen

blood

clinic

sling

L Blends Level 2	flew	black	blueberry	class	clarinet	plug
	fly	blimp	slammer	plane	players	slaw
	play	plaid	plumber	slacks	flying	blue

blimp

flying

Flying on a plane gives dogs jet wag. (jet lag)

plaid

You will wear plaid pants in a play.

class

flew

plumber

A fly flew up your nose.

A plumber is a drain surgeon.

A blue berry is a sad fruit. (blueberry)

Miners eat coal slaw. (coleslaw)

Word Catchers! for Articulation

Copyright © 2004 LinguiSystems, Inc.

blueberry

slammer

A jail for baseball players is a grand slammer.

slacks

Black slacks make you look thinner.

slaw

clarinet

plug

L Blends Level 2	sly	blank	blush	flabby	closet	glitter	glow
	plop	blink	clock	blackboard	clumsy	plump	floor

blackboard

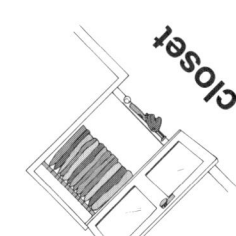

closet

glow

blush

You will glow in the dark.

You will blush when someone winks at you.

flabby

glitter

A plump cat is a flabby tabby.

Red glitter is your favorite glitter color.

A sly fox is hiding in your closet.

Ice cream dropped on the floor is a plop-sicle. (Popsicle)

Word Catchers! for Articulation™

Copyright © 2004 LinguiSystems, Inc.

sly

plop

Your mind will go blank one day.

A clumsy cook spilled the beans.

blank

clumsy

clock

blink

L Blends Level 2	clay	blister	blooming	clever	fluffy	cliff
	flu	glasses	clownfish	flavor	sleigh	float

clay

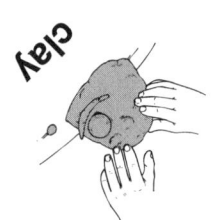

blooming

flavor
Vanilla is your favorite ice-cream flavor.

flu
A sick karate student had the kung flu. (kung fu)

clever
You are very clever.

blister
You will get a blister on your foot.

clownfish
A clownfish does tricks underwater.

fluffy
You like fluffy marshmallows.

glasses

float
You will make a root-beer float.

sleigh
Don't ride a sleigh off a cliff.

cliff

Initial R Level 1	run	ramp	write	ring	room	red	right
	rake	rude	wrong	roof	ruler	rug	

red

run

A bat needs a battery to run.

wrong

You will go to the wrong room.

rug

ruler

Take a ruler to bed to see how long you sleep.

rude

A rude dude will hurt your feelings. The first thing to put in a room is your feet.

Word Catchers! for Articulation™

Copyright © 2004 LinguiSystems, Inc.

write

The paper said to the pen, "Write on!" ("Right on!")

room

rake

You don't need to rake tea leaves.

ramp

You will build a skate ramp.

roof

ring

2

Initial R Level 1	rap	rash	reef	rabbits	row	rose	rid
	rat	read	rest	wrap	rope	wrist	ray

rat

rash

A rope will give you a rash.

Rabbits read books with hoppy endings. (happy endings)

read

wrist

ray

You are as bright as a ray of sunlight.

A present likes wrap music. (rap music)

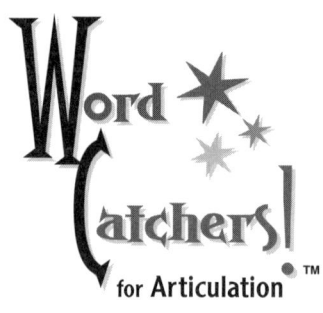

Don't rest in a nap sack. (knapsack)

You will explore a coral reef.

rest

rap

Row, row, row your boat. It's sinking!

Get rid of your bad attitude!

reef

rose

row

rid

rope

Initial R Level 1	rip	raft	real	raise	right	robe	raw
	ram	rain	ride	rhyme	write	rush	

robe

real

A three-dollar bill can't be real.

ride

You will ride on a ram.

rain

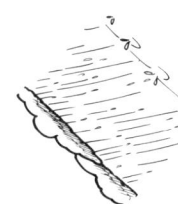

raw

Lions eat raw meat because they can't cook.

rush

You will rush home in the rain.

You will cross the ocean in a raft.

You can write with your right toe.

right

raft

You will write a famous rhyme.

When you raise your arm, your shirt will rip.

rhyme

raise

rip

ram

Initial R Level 1	rod	remind	rivers	rainbow	ranch	rich	rough
	rice	rabbit	robin	rumble	ready	rode	right

rainbow

robin

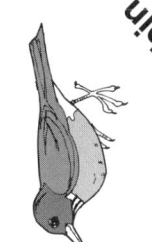

rivers

Lazy rivers never get off their beds.

rode

Batman rode to the store to buy a Robin. (robin)

rod

A car in an oven is a hot rod.

remind

Remind yourself to eat right today.

You will have a rough day.

Fortune cookies won't make you rich.

rough

rich

ready

Are you ready to rumble?

A ranch is never ready because it is dressing.

ranch

rabbit

rice

Initial R Level 1	road	rattle	remote	radio	rescued	wrench	round
	rolls	recess	remove	rocky	robbers	rubber	

radio

rubber

A rubber band doesn't play music.

remove

A dentist will remove one of your teeth.

rolls

round

You deserve a round of applause.

rattle

A baby snake plays with its rattle.

robbers

Robbers are strong because they hold people up.

recess

Your brain is still at recess.

rocky

You will eat rocky-road ice cream.

rescued

You will be rescued from robbers.

remote

wrench

Word Catchers for Articulation

Initial R Level 2	ring	raccoon	radish	rotten	refused	riding	rooster	rises
	ruby	roaring	raisin	robot	wrinkled	range	wrinkle	

rooster

radish

raisin

wrinkle

A raisin is a wrinkled grape.

Don't wrinkle your homework papers.

refused

rises

Your kind offer to a friend will be refused.

A flag rises in the morning and waves all day.

Something smells rotten.

A lion and a crowd were both roaring.

roaring

rotten

A cowboy got hot riding the range.

You will win a ruby ring.

robot

ruby

range

raccoon

Initial R Level 2	relax	raccoon	reason	remark	raven	rubbish	runway
	ride	raincoat	related	reporter	rodeo	roommate	rhino

raincoat

remark

A remark can be caught but not seen.

reporter

A reporter buys a cone to get a scoop.

runway

relax

Relax! Don't worry.

roommate

You will have a raccoon for a roommate.

You are related to someone famous.

You have no reason to complain.

Word Catchers! for Articulation™
Copyright © 2004 LinguiSystems, Inc.

related

reason

rubbish

You will collect rubbish.

You will ride a rhino in a rodeo.

rhino

rodeo

raven

Initial R Level 2	rinse	repeat	rectangle	resort	reptiles	risky
	reply	ribbon	remember	rascal	rowboat	royal

ribbon

repeat
Can you repeat a tongue twister?

rascal
You can be a rascal at times.

reptiles

royal
You will live in a royal palace.

remember
Did you remember to do your homework?

It is risky to chase a skunk.

You will travel to a resort for reptiles.

Copyright © 2004 LinguiSystems, Inc.

rectangle

risky

reply
You will reply to an eek-mail from a mouse. (e-mail)

rinse
Do you rinse and repeat after you use shampoo?

resort

rowboat

Initial R — Level 2

ride	racket	restaurant	racquet	results
rosy	raised	railroad	reunion	roach
route	realize	remover	wreath	wrestle

restaurant

racket

A tennis player raised a racket. (racquet)

railroad

A trainer doesn't ride on a railroad train.

wreath

results

You will get the results you want.

remover

A dog catcher is a Spot remover. (spot remover)

realize

Do you realize how cute you are?

rosy

You have a rosy future.

route

wrestle

You will wrestle a crocodile.

reunion

You will have a family reunion in a zoo.

roach

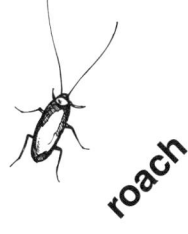

Word Catchers for Articulation
Copyright © 2004 LinguiSystems, Inc.

Initial R Level 2	rug	recipe	rifle	ruffles	resist	Rockies	rely
	rule	relish	rugby	rocket	rusty	recognize	

relish

rocket

rely — Your friends rely on you.

recipe — You have the recipe for success.

rugby — A rug is not for playing rugby.

rule — You rule!

rusty — Don't let your skills get rusty.

resist — It is hard to resist you.

ruffles — A blouse and chips can both have ruffles.

recognize — Someone will recognize your talent.

Rockies

rifle

98

Word Catchers for Articulation
Copyright © 2004 LinguiSystems, Inc.

Medial R Level 1	arms	around	arrow	retired	hurry	garage	dirty
	hero	boring	carrot	everywhere	marry	gorilla	tires

carrot

arms

A clock has two hands but no arms.

A dirty crook steals mud.

dirty

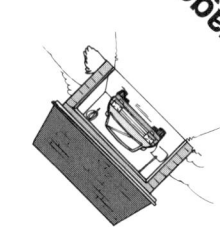

garage

hero

hurry

You will meet your hero.

Old tires are retired.

Copyright © 2004 LinguiSystems, Inc.

Hurry or you will be late.

Belts get around everywhere.

tires

around

gorilla

You will marry a gorilla.

Don't be boring!

marry

boring

arrow

Word Catchers for Articulation
Copyright © 2004 LinguiSystems, Inc.

99

Medial R Level 1	mart	beard	cereal	parade	chirp	shirt	very
	birds	bears	cherry	surprise	horse	story	work

cherry

birds

work

story

Lions work out at a jungle gym.

A story about a horse is a pony tale. (ponytail)

parade

chirp

Bears shop at Cave Mart. (K-Mart)

You will lead a parade.

Birds eat chocolate-chip cookies. (chocolate-chip cookies)

You will find a surprise in a box of cereal.

bears

cereal

shirt

beard

You will never have a bushy beard.

You are getting very, very sleepy.

very

horse

Medial R Level 1	bird	carefully	carpet	early	errors	turkeys	purse	girl
	card	surprise	celery	erase	party	pirate	shark	worm

pirate

celery

carpet

Don't pet a carpet.

party

You will have a surprise party.

girl

You will watch a girl feed a shark.

early

The early bird gets the worm.

A worm took a trip to the Big Apple.

Turkeys don't eat much because they are stuffed.

turkeys

worm

Erase your errors carefully.

Card sharks play games in the ocean.

purse

erase

card

shark

Medial R Level 1	bark	borrow	carry	first	microwaves	tired	turn
	barn	parents	heart	forty	popcorn	turtle	fork

barn

turtle

A turtle can't run away from home.

parents

Listen to your parents.

fork

turn

You will turn right at a fork in a road.

Who will carry you when you are tired?

first

The first man in space was the man in the moon.

You will never hear a tree's bark.

Word Catchers! for Articulation™

Copyright © 2004 LinguiSystems, Inc.

carry

popcorn

Oceans make popcorn in microwaves.

You will borrow some money.

bark

40

forty

borrow

heart

Medial R — Level 2

bury	battery	scary	correct	horse	birdy
bars	address	eerie	perfect	parrot	wordy
Erie	camera	forget	parachute	garden	

camera

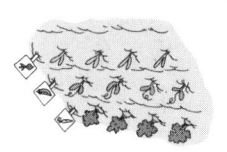
garden

forget — Don't forget to open your parachute.

correct — You always correct your mistakes.

bars — A horse behind bars is a zebra.

eerie — Scary fish live in Lake Eerie. (Lake Erie)

perfect — No one is perfect.

parrot — A parrot is a wordy birdy.

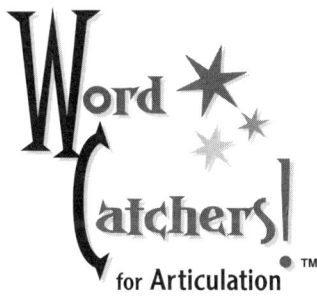
parachute

address — Never wear your address.

bury — Don't bury a dead battery.

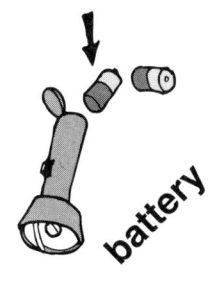
battery

| Medial R Level 2 | park | haircut | macaroni | marbles | parakeet | tourist | works |
| | fired | hornet | cartoon | market | quarters | syrup | |

park
Park your boat in a yacht lot.

fired
A rocket only works when it is fired.

hornet
You will be the lead stinger in a hornet band. (lead singer)

haircut
You will get a great haircut.

tourist
You will meet a tourist in a park.

market
Bugs shop at a flea market.

cartoon
A car watches a cartoon.

quarters
A football game and a dollar have four quarters.

Word Catchers! for Articulation
Copyright © 2004 LinguiSystems, Inc.

Medial R Level 2	horns	Europe	airplane	purple	nursery	work
	herd	farmer	birdseed	giraffe	wearing	tired
	skirt	flowers	hardware	canary	lizard	

airplane

herd — Cows buy tools at a herd-ware store. (hardware store)

tired — You will help a tired farmer.

purple

canary — You planted birdseed to grow a canary.

horns — Cows have bells because their horns don't work.

You will travel to Europe.

You will meet someone wearing a purple skirt.

Word Catchers! for Articulation
Copyright © 2004 LinguiSystems, Inc.

skirt

Europe

You will visit a noisy nursery.

A lizard will follow you home.

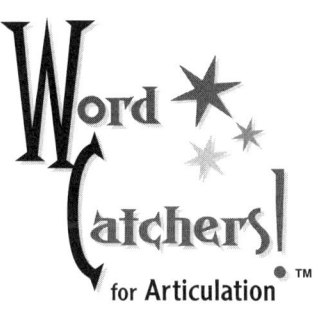

flowers

nursery

lizard

giraffe

Medial R Level 2	word	caterpillar	learn	sparrow	earth
	cargo	thirteen	mirror	airport	gerbil
	carry	Martians	thirty	yourself	larva

thirty

word — A word with one letter is *envelope*.

cargo — You will unload cargo at an airport.

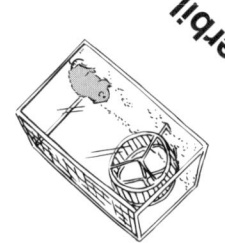

gerbil

thirteen — Thirteen is your lucky number.

carry — You will carry a gerbil to its cage.

learn — You will learn to sing like a sparrow.

yourself — You like to look at yourself in the mirror.

Word Catchers! for Articulation
Copyright © 2004 LinguiSystems, Inc.

larva — A caterpillar had a larva lamp. (lava lamp)

Martians — You will meet thirty Martians.

sparrow

Earth

Final R Level 1	are	bear	never	poor	their	sure	ear
	car	four	where	sore	hear	our	

bear

sore

You will have a sore ear.

Corn has an ear but cannot hear.

hear

four

are

You are going to win a new car.

Where would you like to go on a trip?

poor

You will never have a poor report card.

You can be sure you will succeed.

where

sure

You are one of our finest citizens.

The aliens want their spaceship back.

ear

our

their

car

Final R Level 1	car	after	bear	ever	far	hair	year	her
	jar	chair	door		fire	fur	near	your

door

your

Your hair looks great today.

Don't walk near a fire.

near

fire

her

A ghost in a car must fasten her sheet belt. (seat belt)

year

This will be your lucky year.

Frogs live hoppily ever after. (happily)

You will travel far, far away.

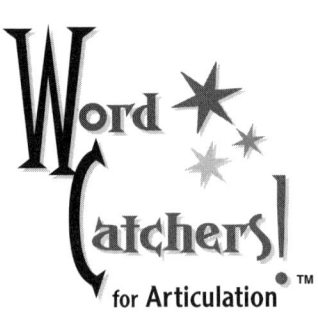

Copyright © 2004 LinguiSystems, Inc.

far

ever

A bear wears a fur coat all year.

You will fall asleep after it is dark.

jar

fur

after

chair

Final R Level 1	are	cheer	deer	fear	scare	stare	pear
	hair	floor	ever	more	shore	tiger	purr

deer

pear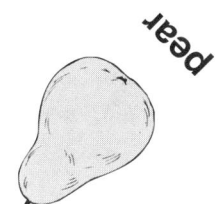

purr

A tiger will purr for you.

You will have more fun today than ever.

more

shore

hair

The shore said, "What's up, dock?" (doc)

Are you having a bad hair day?

Someone will stare at you.

Elephants fear a mouse pad.

Word Catchers! for Articulation™

Copyright © 2004 LinguiSystems, Inc.

stare

fear

A bad trim is a hair scare.

Cheer up!

tiger

cheer

scare

floor

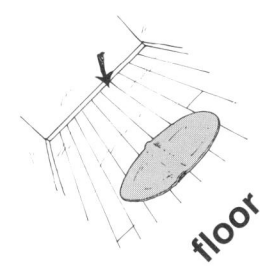

4

Final R Level 1	pear	color	before	never	score	sugar	summer	your
	roar	favor	doctor	zipper	sore	tiger	teacher	over

zipper

over

You will fly over the ocean.

A banana said to a pear, "Let's split."

pear

doctor

favor

Someone will do you a favor.

Blue is your favorite color.

Word Catchers! for Articulation

Copyright © 2004 LinguiSystems, Inc.

Before summer, you will visit the doctor.

A sick lion had a sore roar.

before

roar

color

teacher

Never tease a tiger.

You will score the winning points.

never

score

sugar

110

Word Catchers for Articulation
Copyright © 2004 LinguiSystems, Inc.

Final R Level 1	hair	computer	flower	under	pitcher	father	winner	store
	star	shower	hunter	water	rapper	square	paper	

winner

store

father

pitcher

A happy father is a glad dad.

You will be a star pitcher.

computer

under

A computer can't drive because it keeps crashing.

You will pick a flower under the ocean. (mousse)

A rapper writes songs on wrapping paper.

A hunter put moose in his hair. (mousse)

Word Catchers! for Articulation™

Copyright © 2004 LinguiSystems, Inc.

paper

hunter

shower

A mouse in a shower is squeaky clean.

Water can run but it can't walk.

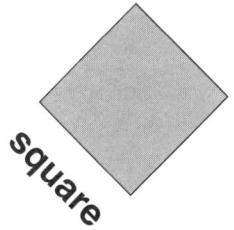

water

square

flower

Final R Level 2	for	alligator	boxer	tractor	sailor	ladder	painter	ruler
	hair	beaver	cooler	farmer	wetter	lecture	saucer	dryer

farmer

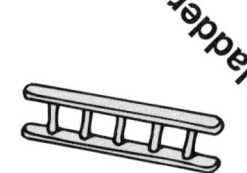

beaver

A beaver told a tree, "Nice gnawing you." (knowing)

sailor

A sailor takes vitamin sea. (C)

ladder

tractor

You will drive a tractor for a farmer.

saucer

You will ride in a flying saucer.

A lecture about the ocean is a beach speech.

You need a cooler ruler.

lecture

cooler

A boxer wears and boxes in a ring.

The opposite of a hair dryer is a toe wetter.

alligator

boxer

dryer

painter

Final R Level 2	tour	weather	butcher	carpenter	longer	your
	her	beware	feather	hamburger	pepper	spider
	her	panther	shredder	newspaper	letter	

pepper

spider

longer

beware

Your bed gets longer when you add your two feet.

Beware of a panther.

feather

letter

Birds watch the feather channel. (weather)

A girl who rips up her mail is a letter shredder.

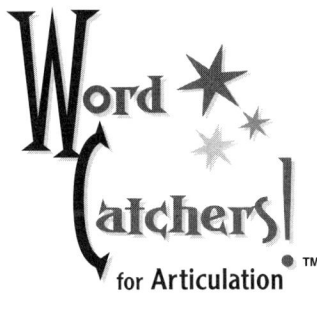

Copyright © 2004 LinguiSystems, Inc.

A butcher dances at a meat ball. (meatball)

You have won a tour of the school.

butcher

tour

A hamburger in a hurry told a bottle to ketchup. (catch up)

A nervous carpenter bites his nails.

panther

hamburger

carpenter

newspaper

Word Catchers for Articulation
Copyright © 2004 LinguiSystems, Inc.

113

Final R Level 2	otter	butter	screwdriver	finger	muffler	molar
	your	umpire	container	harder	temper	for
	solar	faster	haywire	lobster	driver	

umpire

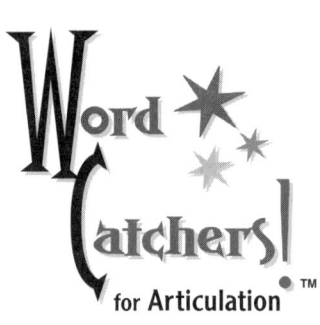

butter

Don't throw butter out the window to see a butterfly.

An apple with a short temper is a crab apple.

temper

finger

haywire

A horse was charged up from eating hay wire. (haywire)

A muffler said, "I am exhausted."

faster

The faster you run, the harder it is to catch your breath.

A driver without a license is a screwdriver.

Word Catchers! for Articulation

Copyright © 2004 LinguiSystems, Inc.

muffler

solar

The sun's back tooth is a solar molar.

A container for ants is a bug jug.

driver

container

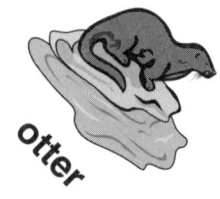

otter

lobster

Final R Level 2	coaster anchor river drummer slower further swatter elevator
	cracker bowler mare nightmare roller gopher whisper

gopher

elevator

An elevator has no feet but runs up and down.

Money goes further the slower you spend it.

slower

anchor

whisper

Someone will whisper to you.

roller

Ghosts ride a roller ghoster. (roller coaster)

A bowler likes to strike out.

The biggest fly swatter is a baseball bat.

Word Catchers! for Articulation™

Copyright © 2004 LinguiSystems, Inc.

swatter

river

A river has a big mouth but doesn't say a word.

A horse that is up late is a night mare. (nightmare)

nightmare

bowler

drummer

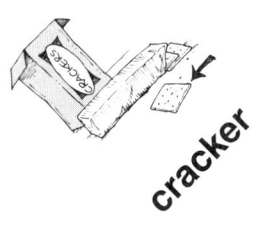

cracker

Final R Level 2

bear	wheelchair	opener	calendar	toaster	polar
more	grandfather	future	shoulder	tinker	timer
fear	grasshopper	wetter	swimmer		

wheelchair

wetter — The more a towel dries, the wetter it gets.

future — Your future is in front of you, but you can't see it.

shoulder

calendar — A calendar said, "I have more dates than you."

grandfather — A grandfather clock is an old timer.

opener — Knights fear a can opener.

grasshopper — A grasshopper is an insect on a pogo stick.

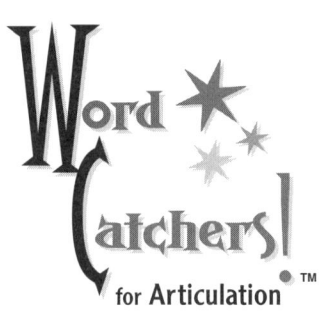

Copyright © 2004 LinguiSystems, Inc.

toaster

polar — You will dance with a polar bear.

stinker — A little skunk grows up to be a big stinker.

swimmer

1

R Blends Level 1	frog	branch	bread	travel	prince	great	draw
	brain	bright	drain	freeway	gravy	green	try

bread

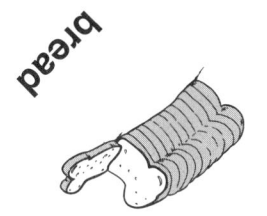

green

travel

Bugs travel on the flea-way. (freeway)

try

You always try your best.

bright

great

A firefly is a bright student.

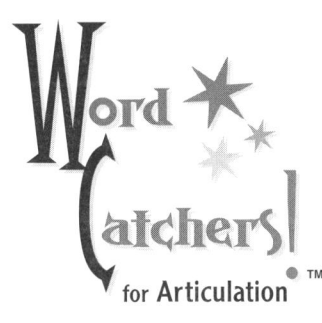

You will have a great day.

You can't travel on a gravy boat.

If you kiss a prince, he will turn into a frog.

gravy

prince

Studying too hard causes a brain drain.

You will draw a great picture.

branch

brain

draw

frog

Word Catchers for Articulation

R Blends Level 1	crab present bride grass eardrum tree grapes groom from
	drum drives broke truck grabby free grouch crown

crown

present

grouch

grass

Sometimes you are a grouch.

When cows cut grass, they moo it. (mow)

free

broke

You will win a free lunch ticket.

Jack couldn't be king because he broke his crown.

Stay away from a grabby crab.

A hog drives a pig-up truck. (pickup truck)

truck

crab

A spider bride and groom had a wedbing. (wedding)

You can't play your ear drum. (eardrum)

tree

groom

drum

grapes

118

R Blends Level 1	grow	break	brown	French	greet	throne	train	fries
	tree	broom	crawl	frights	string	Brooke	tried	tried

brown

French

Monsters order French frights with their burgers. (French fries)

Bees greet each other with a hive five. (high five)

greet

train

throne

A skeleton queen sits on a bone throne.

crawl

A day of shopping is a mall crawl.

You must break an egg before you fry it.

Two witches lived together as broom-mates. (roommates)

Word Catchers! for Articulation™
Copyright © 2004 LinguiSystems, Inc.

broom

Brooke tried to end a fight by wearing make-up.

When you grow up, you will be taller.

break

tree

tried

grow

string

R Blends Level 1	fry	dream	bridge	dress	screen	gray
	true	croak	ground	fruit	Friday	prize
	frog	proud	grandparents	grass		

dress

dream

fry

fruit

You will dream about a gray bridge.

The hottest day is fry day. (Friday)

screen

croak

A screen keeps out bugs and shows movies.

If you eat a frog, you might croak.

Your prize will be a big-screen TV.

Cattle lying on the grass are ground beef.

prize

ground

Your grandparents are proud of you.

You will hear a story that isn't true.

proud

true

gray

bridge

R Blends Level 1	great	dragon	crashed	track	printer	trick
	drop	crayon	grapefruit	trash	trunks	tried
	bring	freeze	driving	treat		

trash

printer

drop

crashed

Don't drop your lemon drop.

A computer crashed on its driving test.

freeze

trick

You can't freeze hot water.

Do you want a trick or a treat?

Someone will bring you great news.

A dragon tried to hide in a crayon box.

bring

crayon

their trunks up.
couldn't keep
elephants
At the pool, the

on the run.
his homework
star does
A track

track

trunks

grapefruit

dragon

1

R Blends Level 2					
drip	drape	grumpy	frosting	screw	crutch
Brent	greets	grizzly	trumpet	straw	from
grape	scratch	cranes	trombone		

screw

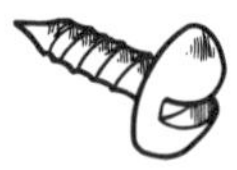

scratch

Chickens bake a cake from scratch.

trumpet

In a jungle band, an elephant plays the trumpet.

straw

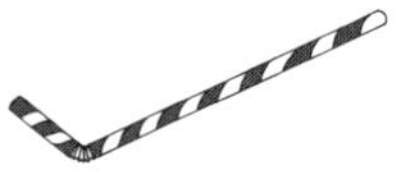

drip

A grumpy faucet said, "You are a drip."

grizzly

A grizzly greets a panda with a bear hug.

Word Catchers! for Articulation™

Brent sits on his watch to be on time.

A skeleton plays the trom-bone. (trombone)

Brent

trombone

If you squeeze a curtain, you get drape juice. (grape)

The loudest birds are whooping cranes.

drape

cranes

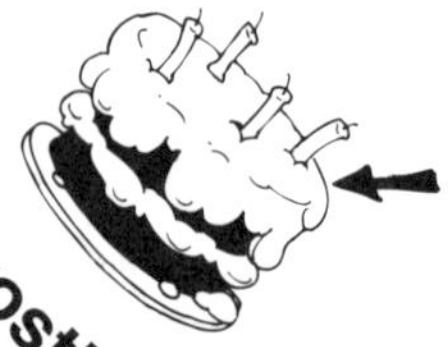

frosting

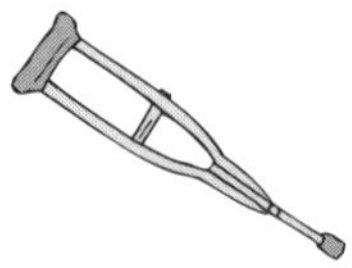

crutch

| R Blends Level 2 | drain
drive
grill | bracelet
breakfast
troubles | bronze
brunch
craving | crossed
present
tricycle | cream
graze
frown |

grill

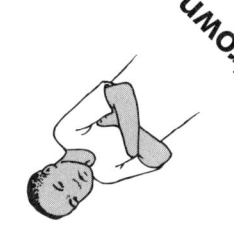

brunch

Brunch is breakfast and lunch.

A computer has a hard drive home.

drive

frown

graze

After cows graze, they go to the moo-vies. (movies)

You are craving ice cream.

crossed

A cow crossed to the udder side. (other side)

A fast tricycle is a tot rod. (hot rod)

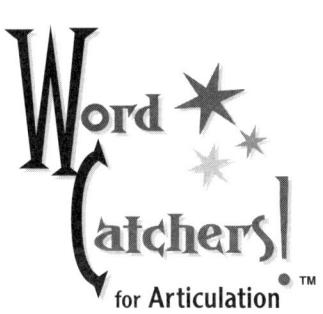

cream

Pour your troubles down the drain.

You will get a bronze bracelet as a present.

tricycle

bracelet

drain

bronze

breakfast

R Blends Level 2

brush	cricket	graduate	pretty	stroke	three
trout	grades	strange	prison	prism	broke
grant	pretzel	triangle	stream		

cricket

pretzel

stroke

strange

You like to stroke your hair.

A strange lady swam in the ocean to get wavy hair.

stream

grant

Don't go trout fishing in a jet stream.

A genie will grant you three wishes.

When the light broke the law, it went to prism. (prison)

You need good grades to graduate.

prism

grades

Bees brush their hair with honey combs. (honeycombs)

A pretty vegetable is a cute-cumber. (cucumber)

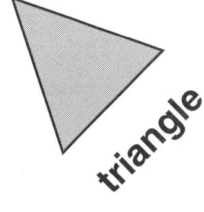

trout

brush

pretty

triangle

R Blends Level 2	groovy	prune	growling	drawers	stroller	dresser	scrub
	crispy	spray	groundhog	treasure	predict	crickets	

groundhog

groovy

You look groovy today.

drawers

A dresser hides when its drawers fall down.

dresser

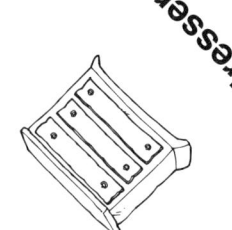

scrub

You will scrub a groundhog.

predict

You can predict the future. Your stomach is growling.

A rabbit uses hare spray. (hair spray)

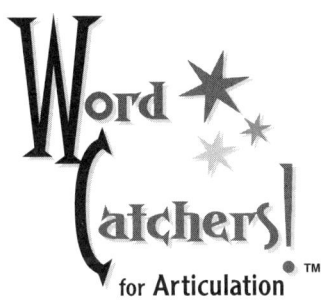

spray

growling

A prune car makes too many pit stops.

You will eat crispy crickets.

stroller

prune

crispy

treasure

5

R Blends Level 2	pro	crashing	practice	pressure	crazy
	frost	creeping	trampoline	scribble	pride
	price	graphs	crocodile	trumpet	

crocodile

pro

crazy Your tire will go crazy from too much pressure.

An ocean is noisy because its waves are crashing. **crashing**

price

You can play a trumpet like a pro.

graphs Two graphs make a paragraph.

A crocodile is creeping up on you.

Copyright © 2004 LinguiSystems, Inc.

Take pride in yourself.

creeping

pride

practice You will practice on a trampoline.

Jack Frost likes to eat chilly. (chili)

scribble

frost

trampoline

Initial SH Level 1	ship	shake	shield	sheep	shock	show
	shoe	shark	should	shine	shop	shy

shark

should

You should travel the ocean in a ship.

shock

A monster's favorite ice cream is shock-olate. (chocolate)

sheep

shop

You will own a shoe shop.

shake

When two strawberries meet, there is a strawberry shake.

You will find your shoe in the foothills.

Word Catchers! for Articulation™

Copyright © 2004 LinguiSystems, Inc.

shy

Sometimes you are shy.

shoe

shine

The sun will shine on you today.

show

A friend will show you the right way.

ship

shield

Initial SH Level 1	chef	shelf	sheets	shirt	shopping	shortcut	shut
	she	shall	should	short	shadow	sugar	sure

shirt

shelf

sure

You are sure of yourself.

shall

You shall be a great ruler.

shut

sugar

If you lick an envelope, it will shut up.

You are so sweet, your name should be Sugar.

A small wound is a short cut. (shortcut)

Bugs go shopping at a flea market.

short

A girl sends a she-mail message. (e-mail)

A messy ghost has dirty sheets.

shopping

chef

she

sheets

shadow

Initial SH Level 1	shot	shade	shampoo	sharks	shouts	shoot
	shy	shake	shaggy	sharp	shovel	shell
	shed	shape	shoulder	shiver		

shade

shampoo

shiver — Sharks make you shiver.

shy — A shy turtle won't come out of its shell.

shouts — A color that shouts is YELL-ow. (yellow)

sharp — You have a sharp mind.

shoot — You will shoot a three-point shot in basketball.

shaggy — A wet, shaggy dog will shake all over you.

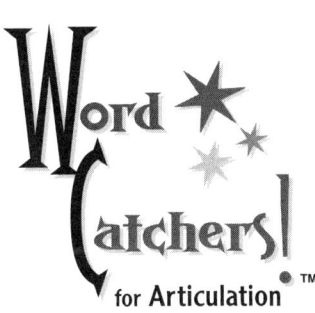

shape — The best place to stay is in shape.

shed — A sewing box is a thread shed.

shovel

shoulder

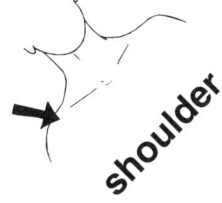

Initial SH Level 2	shack	shore	shocking	shaved	shorts	shop
	ships	sheep	shamrock	shrimp	shove	shrub
	share	shiny	shoulder	shrink		

shrub

shack

shorts — You will wear red shorts.

shrink — Your shorts will shrink in the wash.

share — Two cows share a house in Moo York City. (New York City)

shove — A shove on the shoulder will point you in the right direction. (barbershop)

shaved — Sheep get shaved at the baa-baa shop.

shiny — A shiny dime is still worth ten cents.

shamrock

shore — Loving ships hug the shore.

shocking — The most shocking discovery was electricity.

shrimp

Word Catchers! for Articulation

Copyright © 2004 LinguiSystems, Inc.

Initial SH Level 2	shut	sheepdog	sherbet	shingles	Chicago	shorts	short
	shag	shortcake	sheriff	shoelace	shriek	shush	

sheriff

shut

You must press "Start" to shut down a computer.

Chicago

You will walk a sheepdog in Chicago.

sherbet

shag

You will make a shag rug out of shoelaces.

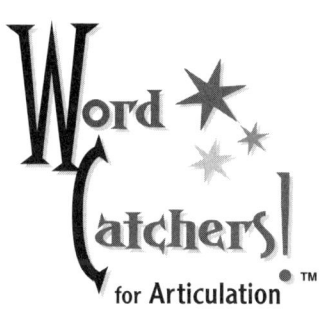

Copyright © 2004 LinguiSystems, Inc.

shorts

You like to wear shorts.

Shingles like to drink roof beer. (root beer)

shush

Shush! Your computer is sleeping.

shortcake

A shortcake is too short to reach the table.

shriek

Little ghosts play hide-and-shriek. (hide-and-seek)

shingles

sheepdog

shoelace

Initial SH Level 2	shawl	shaker	shredded	showed	shortage	shatter	shuttle
	short	shave	shepherd	shower	shortstop	shuffle	

shawl

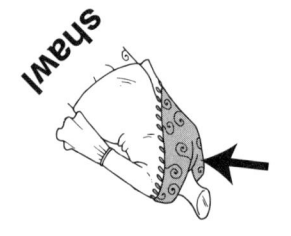

shave

shaker — You need more salt in your shaker.

shortstop — A pig at shortstop plays short-slop.

shortage — You have a cash shortage.

shuttle — You will travel on the space shuttle.

shuffle — You can shuffle cards like a pro.

shredded — Birds eat shredded-tweet cereal. (wheat)

shepherd

shatter — You will shatter a world record.

showed — A bike never showed up because it was two tired. (too tired)

shower

Copyright © 2004 LinguiSystems, Inc.

1

Medial SH Level 1	dishes	finished	machine	station	mushroom	pushy
	ocean	glacier	mashed	wishes	parachute	social

ocean

station

You will live on a space station.

You will step in mashed potatoes.

mashed

parachute

pushy

wishes

A lawn mower likes pushy people.

Your wishes will come true.

You will be a social studies teacher.

You will parachute onto a glacier.

Copyright © 2004 LinguiSystems, Inc.

social

glacier

Is your homework finished?

You will travel in a time machine.

finished

machine

dishes

mushroom

Word Catchers for Articulation
Copyright © 2004 LinguiSystems, Inc.

133

Medial SH — Level 1

mushy	addition	education	seashore	vacation
lotion	brushes	eyelashes	undershirt	washing
bushes	machine	snowshoes		

undershirt

vacation — You will go to the seashore on vacation.

mushy — You will get a mushy kiss.

bushes

lotion — You like lotion that smells like the seashore.

washing — Don't bathe in a washing machine.

brushes — Before an umpire eats, he brushes off his plate.

addition — Addition is heavy work when you have to carry numbers.

eyelashes

education — A good education is important.

seashore — You will live by the seashore.

snowshoes

Medial SH Level 1	bushel	milkshake	tissue	pressure	issue
	fiction	dictionary	special	solution	washer
	fishing	pollution	mansion	tissues	

milkshake

pressure
Don't pressure your parents.

issue
Someone will issue you a fishing license.

fishing
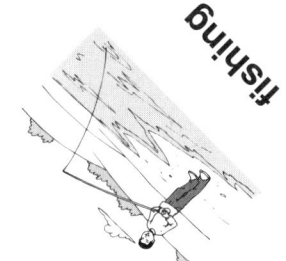

bushel
You can carry a bushel of tissues.

special
You will meet a special friend.

fiction
You will write fiction books.

dictionary
Afternoon comes before morning in the dictionary.

Word Catchers! for Articulation™
Copyright © 2004 LinguiSystems, Inc.

tissue

mansion
You will live in a mansion.

solution
You will find the solution to pollution.

washer

Medial SH Level 2	action	windshield	perfection	anxious	ashore
	fishy	wishbone	satisfaction	washed	cashier
	ashes	fractions	washcloth		

wishbone

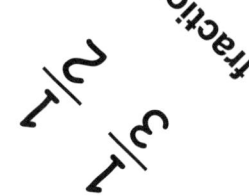

cashier

A cashier will give you too much change.

satisfaction

Satisfaction comes from the satis-factory. (satisfactory)

fractions

$\frac{1}{2}$ $\frac{1}{3}$

anxious

An anxious horse swallowed a dollar bill and bucked.

A sailor's dirty clothes can be washed ashore.

ashore

action

You will star in an action movie.

A log told some ashes, "You're fired!"

ashes

washcloth

perfection

You are close to perfection.

A sardine's story sounds fishy to you.

fishy

windshield

Medial SH Level 2	Sasha	flashlight	cashing	commercial	seashell
	unsure	musician	caution	marshmallow	sessions
	cushion	national	fashion	mission	

seashell

cashing
You will be cashing big checks.

musician
You will be a jazz musician and play in jam sessions.

flashlight

mission

You will have a difficult mission.

You will be a national champion.

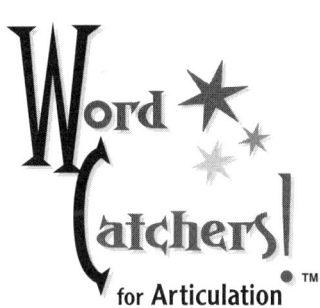
Copyright © 2004 LinguiSystems, Inc.

Sasha
You will go on a secret mission with Sasha.

Use caution when you are unsure.

national

cushion

commercial
You will star in a national TV commercial.

fashion
You will be a fashion model.

caution

marshmallow

Medial SH Level 2	cashew	fisherman	location	pollution	slingshot	mention
	sushi	information	sunshine	rushing	snapshot	tension

snapshot

information

Don't share secret information.

You won't find any cash in a cashew.

cashew

sunshine

sushi

You will eat sushi for lunch.

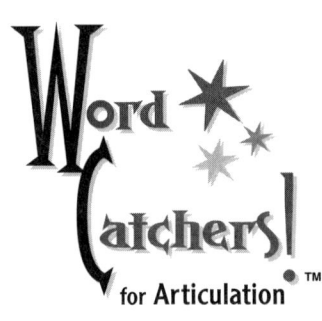

You will mention something important in class.

location

You will move to a new location.

Too much tension makes you tense.

mention

tension

You will help clean up pollution.

You do a lot of rushing around.

pollution

fisherman

rushing

slingshot

| Final SH Level 1 | ash | blush | trash | leash | foolish | fish | splish |
| | cash | crash | hush | polish | splash | wish | |

leash

trash

foolish — A baby ant feels foolish. All of his uncles are ants. (aunts)

hush — You can stop a barking dog with hush puppies.

ash — A fireplace said, "If you want something, ash for it." (ask for it)

polish — Elephants wear green nail polish to hide in a pea patch.

wish — What would you wish for?

blush — Someone will make you blush.

splash — Splish, splash, a fish is sneaking up behind you.

crash — If you crash into a cow, moo-ve it out of the way. (move)

cash

fish

Word Catchers! for Articulation

Copyright © 2004 LinguiSystems, Inc.

Final SH Level 1	bush	brush	jellyfish	Josh	slosh	dish	rush
	dash	flash	starfish	push	smash	swish	

smash

slosh

starfish

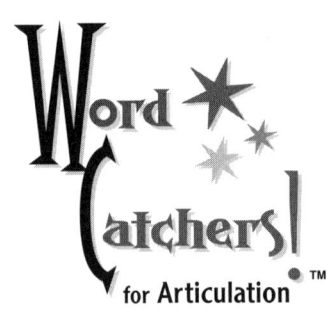

brush

swish

Josh will slosh through the snow to find you.

A mermaid cleans house for a starfish.

push

You will swish a basketball through the hoop.

A firefly said, "My battery is dead. Give me a push."

A jellyfish cuts through waves with a sea-saw.

You will make a mad dash for the lunch line.

dash

jellyfish

You are in a rush to grow up.

You can do your homework in a flash.

dish

rush

flash

bush

Final SH Level 1	gosh	English	crash	ticklish	finish	rush	fish
	Irish	eyelash	crush	goldfish	selfish	wash	

crash

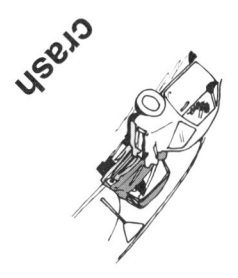

selfish

You are not selfish. You care about others.

rush

A cow in a rush forgot her beef-case. (briefcase)

eyelash

crush

Someone has a crush on you.

wash

Fish wash in a bass-tub. (bathtub)

You will teach English to goldfish.

Gosh, you have an eyelash on your cheek.

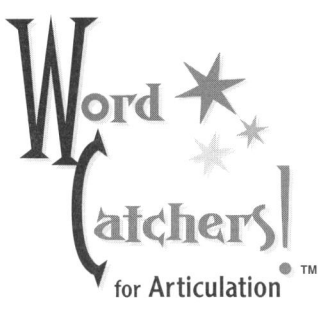

Copyright © 2004 LinguiSystems, Inc.

gosh

English

You are very ticklish.

You will learn an Irish dance.

finish

ticklish

Irish

goldfish

Final SH Level 2	bash	childish	flush	Spanish	radish	sash
	lush	sawfish	fresh	toothbrush	stylish	slush

slush

lush — Watch out for a lush patch of poison ivy.

Spanish — You will speak Spanish on the radio.

fresh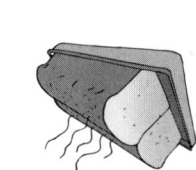

childish — It's okay to be childish once in a while.

stylish — Stylish bears wear fur coats.

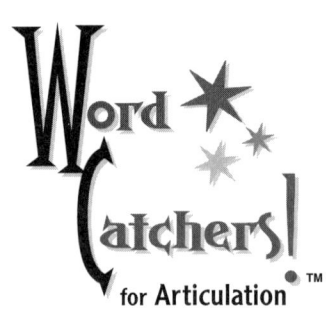

flush — A toilet was starting to flush.

bash — Someone is planning a birthday bash for you!

radish

sawfish — You saw a sawfish but it never saw you.

sash — You will wear a sash that says "Misunderstood."

toothbrush

Final SH — Level 2

brush	licorice	mouthwash	pinkish	vanish
plush	catfish	paintbrush	punish	push
clash	rosebush	sagebrush	refresh	mash

catfish

sagebrush — Sagebrush is not a brush for spices.

vanish — When you stand up, your lap will vanish.

mouthwash

refresh — A computer will feel better after you push *refresh*.

punish — A teacher will punish a chick that cheeps on a test. (cheats)

mash — Potatoes don't like the word *mash*.

plush — A plush blanket said to the bed, "I've got you covered."

licorice — Never wear a licorice bracelet.

clash — Do blue eyes clash with a pinkish shirt?

rosebush

paintbrush

Final SH Level 2	relish	accomplish	swordfish	rubbish	trash	fish
	squash	extinguish	hogwash	goulash	wash	ash
	marsh	hairbrush	mustache	sunfish		

hairbrush

goulash

Ghouls' favorite food is ghoul-ash. (goulash)

squash

If you throw a pumpkin, it comes down squash.

marsh

rubbish

A joke about trash is rubbish.

sunfish

The brightest fish is a sunfish.

extinguish

Don't call a firefighter to extinguish a firefly.

Word Catchers! for Articulation
Copyright © 2004 LinguiSystems, Inc.

hogwash

Pigs doing laundry is hog wash. (hogwash)

relish

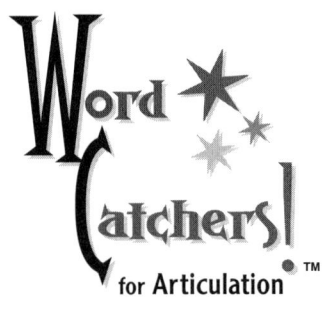

accomplish

You will accomplish many things.

swordfish

Knights in armor eat swordfish.

mustache

Initial CH Level 1	chair	chance	charm	chicken	China	checkers	chop	chirp
	chew	charge	cheap	cheese	chomp	chocolate	chip	

chicken

chomp — A lion can chomp anywhere it wants.

chop — You will chop a tree down and then chop it up.

chair

charm — You will win a charm bracelet.

chew — You will sell bubblegum on a chew-chew train. (choo-choo)

charge — Used batteries are free of charge.

cheap — You are so cheap that you don't pay attention.

checkers

chance — You will have a chance to visit China.

chocolate — A bird likes chocolate-chirp cookies. (chocolate-chip)

chirp

cheese

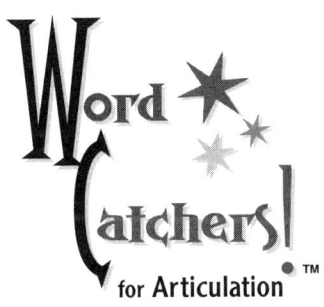

Word Catchers! for Articulation
Copyright © 2004 LinguiSystems, Inc.

Initial CH Level 1	chin	chalk	changing	channel	cheek
	chili	chilly	chickens	cheater	Chile
	chain	chase	children	chosen	chimp

chalk

chain

cheek
Someone will pinch your cheek.

chilly
The opposite of a hot dog is a chilly dog. (chili)

chili
You will knit sweaters for chillybeans. (chili)

chase
A chimp will chase you after school.

changing
You are changing all the time.

channel
Chickens watch the feather channel. (weather)

children

chosen
You will be chosen for a trip to Chile.

cheater
Don't play cards with a cheater.

chin

Initial CH Level 1	check	chunky	checkers	choice	champ
	cheer	change	chocolate	choose	chick
	chips	Charles	chipmunk	chubby	chores

check

chips

choose

A chipmunk will choose you to play with.

chick

Don't feed a baby chick potato chips.

chunky

You like chocolate chips in chunky peanut butter.

chipmunk

You will spot a chubby chipmunk.

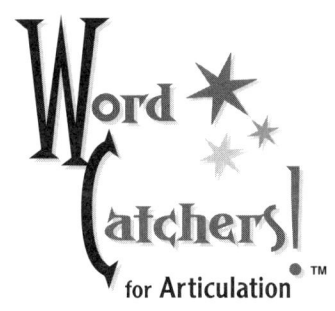

You will be a checkers champ.

A great singer has a choice voice.

champ

choice

change

cheer

A cheer for carrots is "Raw, raw!" (rah, rah)

chores

You will do your chores well.

Charles

Initial CH Level 2

cello	chapter	champion	chuckle	chatty
chat	cherish	cheeseburger	cheerful	chess
Chad's	cheetah	chocolate		

cello

cheetah

Chad's — Chad's cheetah will eat your cheeseburger.

cherish — You will cherish your pet cheetah.

cheerful — You are a cheerful person.

chocolate — Your dentist will give you a chocolate filling.

chuckle — You make your friends chuckle.

champion — You will be a chess champion.

Word Catchers! for Articulation
Copyright © 2004 LinguiSystems, Inc.

chapter — You will read an exciting chapter in a book.

chatty — You are too chatty in class.

chat

cheeseburger

Initial CH Level 2	chess chili China	chairman charming chimpanzee	chatter chicks Chile	chipmunks chopsticks chopping	chipped Chinese

chess

charming

You will meet Prince Charming.

Chipmunks will chatter to you today.

chatter

chopsticks

chairman

You will be chairman of the bored. (board)

You will use chopsticks in China.

China

A chimpanzee used a monkey wrench to escape from a zoo.

chimpanzee

chicks

Some computers chipped in for a vacation to Chile.

chipped

Chinese

You will learn to speak Chinese.

A lumberjack buys food at the chopping center. (shopping)

chopping

chili

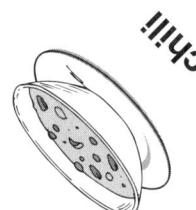

Word Catchers! for Articulation
Copyright © 2004 LinguiSystems, Inc.

Initial CH Level 2

Chet	charcoal	checkers	chessboard	chicken	chimney
cheese	cheeks	cheddar	chewing	choppy	chummy
chaps	checkbook	cheetah	challenge		

chaps

chummy

cheddar

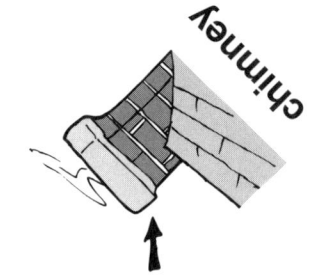

chimney

Don't get too chummy with a cheetah.

A mouse wants your cheddar cheese.

choppy

chewing

A lazy ax had a choppy room. (sloppy room)

You will step in chewing gum.

A chicken will give you a checkbook.

Chet will challenge you to a game of checkers.

checkbook

Chet

You will face a difficult challenge.

You will play checkers on a chessboard.

charcoal

challenge

chessboard

cheeks

Medial CH Level 1	itches	crutches	ketchup	watchdog	richer
	catcher	fortune	beaches	sandwiches	future
	creature	stretches	peaches	scratching	

ketchup

catcher

future

You have a bright future.

Rubber is the longest word because it stretches.

stretches

creature

beaches

You will go swimming with a sea creature.

You will find treasure on two beaches.

Adorable peaches are cute fruits.

Don't hurt yourself by scratching your itches too hard.

peaches

scratching

Eating fortune cookies won't make you richer.

A watchdog can tell time.

sandwiches

fortune

watchdog

crutches

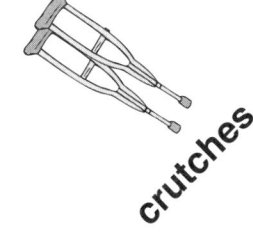

Medial CH Level 1	batches	catching	butchers	watches	watching	richest
	kitchen	grouchy	lunchroom	question	nachos	inches

kitchen

batches — You will eat two batches of nachos.

catching — You are catching a cold.

watches

lunchroom — A computer went in the lunchroom for a mega-byte. (bite)

watching — Halloween night is witch watching.

question — Someone wants to ask you a question.

grouchy — Sometimes you are grouchy.

butchers — Butchers dance at the meat ball. (meatball)

richest — The richest nuts are cash-ews. (cashews)

inches

nachos

Medial CH Level 1	achieve	hatching	pasture	armchair	sketches
	itches	lunchbox	pitcher	touchdown	teacher
	fetches	munchies	rancher	picture	

teacher

touchdown — You will score a touchdown.

munchies — You will have munchies for lunch.

pitcher

achieve — You will achieve great things.

lunchbox — Your picture will be on a lunchbox.

itches — If your nose itches, you will kiss a fool.

pasture — A mother cow said, "It is pasture bedtime." (past your)

Word Catchers! for Articulation
Copyright © 2004 LinguiSystems, Inc.

fetches — An artistic dog fetches and sketches.

rancher — A rancher reads the daily moos-paper. (newspaper)

hatching

armchair

Medial CH Level 2

archery	enchanted	marching	kitchen	mixture
inches	microchips	orchard	hatchet	patches
nature	inchworm	purchase		

hatchet

inches
You will grow two inches this year.

mixture
You will create a tasty mixture in the kitchen.

archery

purchase
You will purchase a new computer.

enchanted
You will walk through an enchanted forest.

orchard
You will be as happy as a worm in an apple orchard.

microchips
Hungry computers eat microchips.

inchworm

patches
Fix broken pumpkins with pumpkin patches.

nature
You will be a nature guide.

marching

Medial CH Level 2	statue	matches	bleachers	duchess	vulture
	itchy	poncho	dogcatcher	teacher	witches
	mature	puncture	situations		

bleachers

puncture

witches

vulture

A fork in a road will puncture your tire.

Two little witches failed spelling class.

situations

itchy

You get out of sticky situations easily.

Watching a vulture makes you itchy all over.

You will win three checkers matches.

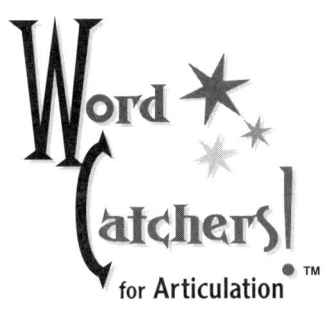
Copyright © 2004 LinguiSystems, Inc.

You will make mature decisions.

matches

mature

A dogcatcher will be your teacher for one day.

You will meet a duchess in your neighborhood.

duchess

dogcatcher

poncho

statue

Medial CH Level 2

mischief	cockroaches	bachelor	highchair	Rachel
stitches	temperature	enchilada	signature	roaches
reaching	woodchucks	furniture		

enchilada

cockroaches

woodchucks

highchair

signature

Clock-roaches can tell you the time. (cockroaches)

Do woodchucks really chuck wood?

Rachel

Your signature will be valuable one day.

Rachel has an enchilada for you.

Word Catchers! for Articulation
Copyright © 2004 LinguiSystems, Inc.

You will get into some mischief.

You will get new furniture soon.

mischief

furniture

(bachelor)
bat-chelor.
bat is a
An unmarried

outside.
temperature
a warm
You like

stitches

bachelor

temperature

reaching

Final CH Level 1	each	beach	couch	crunch	pinch	speech	watch	wrench
	much	peach	lunch	grouch	punch	branch	witch	

peach

punch
A boxer's favorite drink is punch.

each
You will laugh each and every day.

couch

witch
A witch tells time with a witch watch. (wrist watch)

You can't have too much fun.

crunch
You crunch too much at lunch.

A talk on the beach is a beach speech.

Word Catchers! for Articulation
Copyright © 2004 LinguiSystems, Inc.

much

grouch
A grouch will call you tonight.

pinch
A lobster playing baseball is a pinch hitter.

beach

branch

wrench

Final CH Level 1	itch catch crutch scratch search such
	rich coach ditch sandwich reach teach

coach

reach
A singer stood on a ladder to reach high notes.

itch
Scratch paper makes you itch.

scratch

ditch

rich
You will be very rich.

You will teach in a ditch.

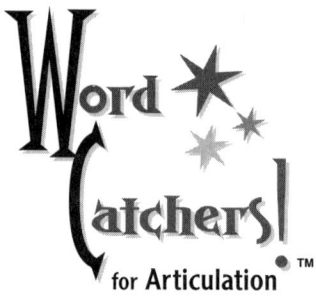

You are such a nice person.

A glove said to a ball, "Catch you later."

such

search
You will search for lost animals.

You will teach others to make a great sandwich.

catch

teach

crutch

sandwich

Final CH Level 1	inch	bench	March	sketch	smooch	switch
	ouch	birch	ranch	slouch	stretch	watch

watch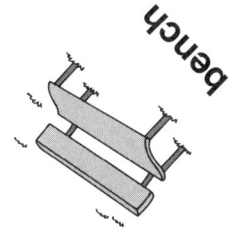

stretch

Stretch before you exercise.

smooch

Cows in love like to smooo-ch. (smooch)

bench

March

The middle of *March* is *r*.

Don't slouch. Sit up straight.

inch

You will grow an inch next month.

You will live on a ranch and eat ranch dressing.

slouch

ranch

sketch

switch

A light wants to switch with you.

That birch tree is tree-mendous. (tremendous)

birch

ouch

Final CH Level 2

hatch	drench	hopscotch	bleach	lunch	pitch
cinch	French	research	twitch	match	pouch
couch	speech	launch	leech		

hopscotch

match

cinch

launch

Hopscotch is a cinch for you.

An astronaut's favorite meal is launch. (lunch)

pouch

drench

A lazy baby kangaroo is a pouch potato. (couch potato)

You drench your French fries with ketchup.

You will pitch a perfect baseball game.

research

You will do research about the leech.

pitch

Word Catchers! for Articulation
Copyright © 2004 LinguiSystems, Inc.

bleach

twitch

You twitch when you sleep.

hatch

An egg and an idea both hatch.

speech

Final CH Level 2	arch patch butterscotch torch which
	batch clench church touch watch
	bunch scorch stench French

bunch

torch

which

clench

Which wristwatch do you want?

You clench your teeth when you think.

patch

scorch

You will take a nap in a strawberry patch.

You will scorch your supper on fry day. (Friday)

Word Catchers! for Articulation™
Copyright © 2004 LinguiSystems, Inc.

A skunk's favorite snack is stench fries. (French fries)

You will eat a batch of butterscotch cookies.

stench

batch

A dog that swallows a wrist watch gets lots of ticks.

Don't touch a torch that is lit.

arch

wristwatch

touch

church

Final CH Level 2	finch	brunch	French	ostrich	pooch	snatch	stitch
	munch	enrich	glitch	spinach	porch	watch	

finch

ostrich

porch

An ostrich is sitting on your porch.

glitch

You will lose your data in a power glitch.

spinach

Spiders eat spinach and French flies. (French fries)

brunch

Don't fix brunch. It isn't broken.

enrich

A good book will enrich your day.

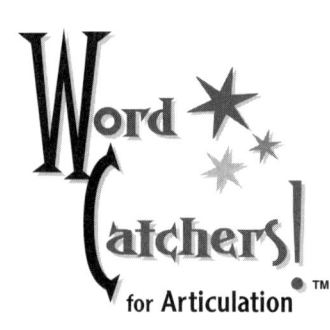

munch

You like to munch while you watch TV.

snatch

Someone will try to snatch your French fries.

pooch

A pooch washes its clothes at a laundro-mutt. (Laundromat)

French

stitch

Initial J Level 1	gem	germ	jail	jog	join	jump	jam
	gym	jack	jeans	joy	juice	June	jay

jack

gym

You will find a gem in a gym.

When mice jog, they wear squeakers. (sneakers)

jog

juice

germ

A germ crossed a microscope to get to the other slide. (side)

jay

A J is a letter of the alphabet that can fly. (jay)

join

A bee will join a band to be the lead stinger. (lead singer)

jam

You will eat jam and bread for lunch.

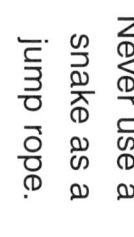

Word Catchers! for Articulation™
Copyright © 2004 LinguiSystems, Inc.

jail

jump

Never use a snake as a jump rope.

You will jump for joy in June.

June

jeans

Initial J Level 1	jab	Jake	jig	jets	junk	joy
	jar	jazz	job	joke	just	jug

jets

just

Just hum if you don't know the words.

junk

Your job will be to collect junk.

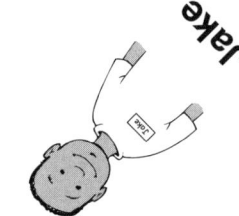

Jake

jig

You will do a jig with a pig.

joke

Never tell a joke when you are skating. The ice might crack up.

jab

A stranger will jab your arm by mistake.

jazz

A jazz singer stood on a ladder so she could hit the high notes.

job

Your first job will be great!

joy

You were once a bundle of joy.

jug

jar

Initial J Level 1	June	genie	genius	jellybeans	giraffe	giant
	July	jerky	jumped	jellyfish	juggle	jeans
	jury	jiggle	journey	jungle		

jacket

giant

You will watch a giant juggle.

A genie will take you on a journey.

journey

jungle

jury

jellyfish

You will be on a jury in June.

You will eat jellybeans in July.

The peanut butter jumped into the ocean to be with a jellyfish.

A nervous cow is beef jerky.

Word Catchers! for Articulation

Copyright © 2004 LinguiSystems, Inc.

July

genius

A genius in jeans is wearing smarty pants.

Never jiggle in the jungle.

jerky

jiggle

giraffe

genie

Initial J Level 2	Japan	genuine	jackal	jellybeans	Jupiter	jockey	journey
	jolly	January	jaguar	jitterbug	jukebox	junior	

jellybeans

jaguar

jockey

junior

A jockey wears saddle shoes.

A jaguar named Junior will follow you home.

January

jitterbug

You will travel to Jupiter in January.

A jitterbug is like a playing card because it belongs to a pack.

You will have a jolly journey.

A jitterbug is a nervous insect.

jolly

jackal

You think that jellybeans are a genuine vegetable.

You will play a song on a jukebox in Japan.

Jupiter

genuine

Japan

jukebox

2

Initial J Level 2	Judy's	generous	ginger	janitor	jeweler	joker	gingersnaps
	jelly	journal	joyful	jealous	jewels	juggle	

juggle

janitor
A janitor will sweep you off your feet.

You will be a jeweler with many jewels.
jeweler

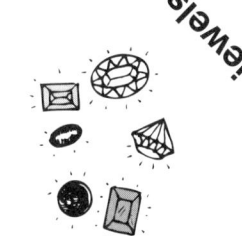
jewels

generous
You are so generous, you gave away your lunch.

jealous
You are jealous of deer hunters because they have lots of bucks.

Word Catchers! for Articulation™
Copyright © 2004 LinguiSystems, Inc.

Be careful picking flowers because the ginger snaps. (gingersnaps)
ginger

You should keep a journal.
journal

Judy's vegetable necklace is a food chain.
Judy's

You have a joyful giggle.
joyful

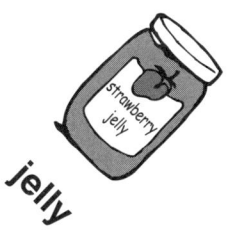
jelly

joker

Initial J Level 2	gym	general	jiggling	javelin	gelatin	Jordan
	giant	gentle	jackknife	jaywalk	jumping	jersey
	jumbo	Georgia	Jamaica	jabber		

giant

general

jabber

You jabber too much in gym class.

gentle

You will travel to Jamaica with a gentle giant.

jumbo

"Jumbo shrimp" doesn't make sense.

Jamaica

Jamaica has friendly boats that hug the shore.

Jordan

Messy Jordan wrote his report with a pig pen. (pigpen)

jersey

You will buy a red jersey in New Jersey.

jackknife

jaywalk

Don't jaywalk in Georgia.

gelatin

You like jumping, jiggling gelatin.

javelin

Medial J Level 1	agent	bandages	judges	stagecoach	magician	soldier
	magic	engaged	pageant	refrigerator	margarine	injury

magician

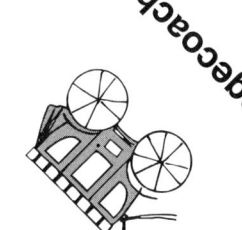

stagecoach

refrigerator — A witch in a refrigerator casts a cold spell.

bandages — Doctor Smith keeps bandages in the refrigerator for cold cuts.

agent — You are really a secret agent.

judges — Judges and English teachers both hand out long sentences.

engaged — An engaged woman is like a phone. They both have rings.

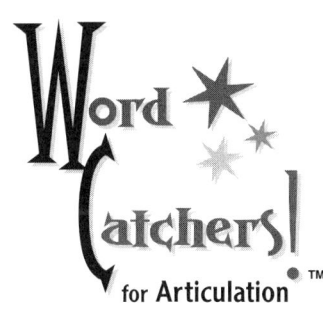

Word Catchers! for Articulation
Copyright © 2004 LinguiSystems, Inc.

injury — A small injury is a short cut. (shortcut)

magic — You will become a magician and make magic.

pageant — You will win a beauty pageant.

margarine

soldier

Medial J Level 1	magic	teenagers	oranges	pigeon	sergeant	stingy
	banjo	vegetable	stranger	bridges	angelfish	danger

banjo

teenagers — You will play the banjo with teenagers.

danger — Danger is your middle name.

bridges

stranger — Beware of a stranger.

oranges — You like juicy oranges.

vegetable — Your favorite vegetable is popcorn.

stingy — You are not stingy with your money.

Word Catchers! for Articulation
Copyright © 2004 LinguiSystems, Inc.

oranges

sergeant — An army dentist is a drill sergeant.

magic — You will learn a magic trick.

stingy

angelfish

pigeon

Medial J Level 1	angel	engine	badger	legend	ranger	object
	cages	gadget	pajamas	project	subject	edges

pajamas

angel

You try to be an angel.

You will travel to the edges of a galaxy.

edges

cages

object

You will ride on a flying object.

A forest ranger will rescue you.

project

You have a project that is due.

Lunch is your best subject.

Word Catchers! for Articulation
Copyright © 2004 LinguiSystems, Inc.

ranger

subject

You are a legend in your own mind.

You will invent a new gadget.

engine

legend

gadget

badger

Medial J Level 2

oxygen	astrologer	passenger	squeegee	injection
dungeon	dangerous	flapjacks	tangerine	engineer
original	endangered	hydrogen		

dungeon

passenger
You will be a passenger on a spaceship.

original
Your artwork is original.

astrologer
An astrologer holds up his pants with an asteroid belt.

tangerine

endangered
You will help endangered animals.

flapjacks
You flip over flapjacks.

dangerous
A dictionary is dangerous because it has dynamite in it.

injection
An injection for a rocket is a booster shot.

oxygen
Water is made of oxygen and hydrogen.

engineer

squeegee

Word Catchers! for Articulation™
Copyright © 2004 LinguiSystems, Inc.

Medial J Level 2	Egypt	adjust	eligible	tragedy	region	major
	aging	digits	suggest	hedgehog	register	Roger

major

Egypt

region

adjust

You will live in another region.

Could you adjust to living in Egypt?

aging

digits

You are aging right now.

Hands and phone numbers have digits.

You are not eligible to be a major yet.

Copyright © 2004 LinguiSystems, Inc.

You will pet a hedgehog named Roger.

Roger

eligible

hedgehog

tragedy

suggest

register

I see no tragedy in your future.

I suggest you study more.

Medial J Level 2	ajar	apologize	budget	enjoy	scavenger	fragile	reject
	eject	Bridget	charging	fidget	geologist	urgent	

fragile

urgent
You will get an urgent message.

fidget
You fidget too much in class.

geologist

scavenger

reject

You enjoy scavenger hunts.

You will reject a bad idea.

Bridget wants to be a geologist.

A door is not a door when it is ajar. (a jar)

Bridget

ajar

budget

Someone will apologize to you.

Don't press *eject* in a jet.

apologize

eject

charging

Final J Level 1	age	badge	fudge	judge	orange	cage
	page	charge	grudge	large	sponge	stage

badge

page

A page sleeps under a book cover.

Someone will give you orange pajamas.

orange

sponge

stage

You will play a sponge on the stage.

charge

You are large and in charge.

grudge

You are holding a grudge against someone.

judge

You will judge a pie-eating contest.

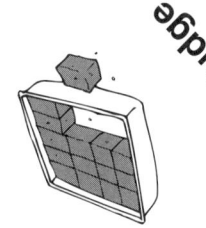

fudge

large

You will need a large cage for a pet.

You don't look your age.

age

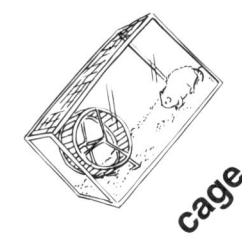

cage

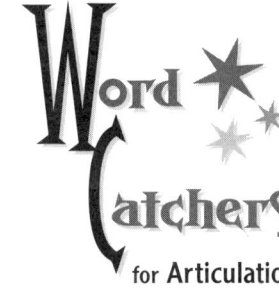

Copyright © 2004 LinguiSystems, Inc.

Final J Level 1	age	barge	bridge	huge	strange	ledge	range
	edge	hedge	change	rage	lounge	nudge	

bridge

edge

Don't stand on the edge of a ledge.

You like to lounge.

lounge

change

nudge

Never nudge a porcupine.

huge

A huge ant is an eleph-ant. (elephant)

A chef in a rage beat the eggs and whipped the cream.

It is strange that your age goes up and never comes down.

strange

rage

You will throw a clock off the ledge to see time fly.

If you live in the hills, you will cook food on a mountain range.

ledge

range

barge

hedge

Final J Level 1	college	beverage	garbage	luggage	message	page
	garage	cabbage	language	marriage	village	voyage

luggage

message

college

garbage

You will find a message in a bottle.

You will go to college for ten years.

garage

village

A car that runs on peanut butter sticks to the roof of the garage.

You will take a voyage on the *Titanic*.

You will live in a village made of garbage.

A cabbage has a head but no brain.

Word Catchers! for Articulation™

Copyright © 2004 LinguiSystems, Inc.

voyage

cabbage

Billboards talk to each other in sign language.

You will spill a beverage on your new clothes.

page

language

beverage

marriage

Final J Level 2	urge	average	cottage	damage	package	sausage	pledge
	image	carriage	courage	manage	revenge	wreckage	

package

sausage

average

revenge

You are above average.

Someone wants revenge.

urge

courage

You have an urge to dance.

A hen needed courage because she was chicken.

Nervous wreckage shakes on the bottom of the ocean.

You will eat cottage cheese for lunch.

wreckage

cottage

A bad mistake could damage your image.

You will manage a professional basketball team.

pledge

damage

manage

carriage